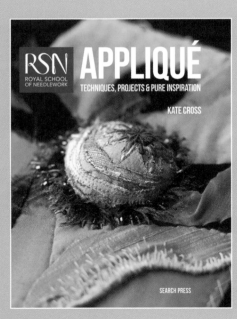

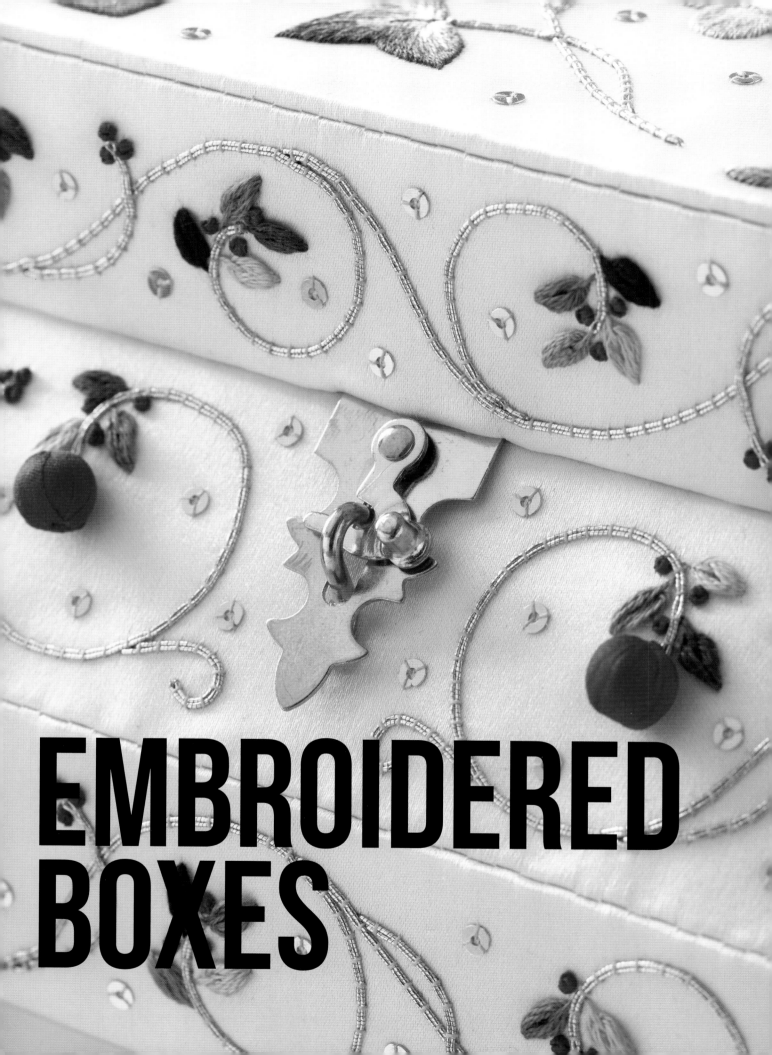

EMBROIDERED BOXES

DEDICATION

To my wonderful husband, Richard, my soulmate, who encouraged me throughout even though I made his life a constant challenge in dodging my piles of stuff.

To my children, Isabella and Jack, for their love and support during the stitching for and writing of this book and especially for their help in finding my many pins in the carpet!

To my parents, who encouraged me to study on the RSN apprenticeship, for their ongoing support.

Finally, to my grandmother who, back in the 1980s, introduced me to needlework, and sadly will never see this in print.

ACKNOWLEDGEMENTS

I would like to thank the Royal School of Needlework, which offered me this opportunity; I had forgotten just how much I love box-making.

To all my friends, colleagues and students at the Royal School of Needlework who provide great inspiration; and especially Margaret Dier for her support and guidance.

I would also like to thank Kate Barlow, Lisa Bilby, Rachel Doyle, Nikki Fairhurst, Sara Rickards and Deborah Wilding for allowing their work to be photographed.

Finally, I would like to thank Paul Bricknell for taking such wonderful photographs and special thanks to my editor, Beth Harwood, for her patience and support.

First published in 2020

Search Press Limited
Wellwood, North Farm Road,
Tunbridge Wells, Kent TN2 3DR

Reprinted 2021

Text and illustrations copyright © Heather Lewis 2020

Photographs by Paul Bricknell at Search Press Studios

Design copyright © Search Press Ltd 2020

ISBN: 978-1-78221-652-0

Suppliers
For details of suppliers, please visit the Search Press website:
www.searchpress.com

For more information about the RSN, its courses, studio, shop and exhibitions, see: www.royal-needlework.org.uk

For information about the RSN degree programme, see:
www.rsndegree.uk

EMBROIDERED BOXES

HEATHER LEWIS

TECHNIQUES, PROJECTS & PURE INSPIRATION

SEARCH PRESS

CONTENTS

RSN THE ROYAL SCHOOL OF NEEDLEWORK

ROYAL SCHOOL OF NEEDLEWORK
Founded 1872

Founded in 1872, the Royal School of Needlework (RSN) is the international centre of excellence for the art of hand embroidery. It is based at Hampton Court Palace in west London but also offers courses across the UK, in the USA and Japan. Today it is a thriving, dynamic centre of teaching and learning, and believes that hand embroidery is a vital art form that impacts on many aspects of our lives from clothes to ceremonial outfits, and from home furnishings to textile art.

To enable and encourage people to learn the skill of hand embroidery the RSN offers courses from beginner to degree level. The wide range of short courses includes introductions to each of the stitch techniques the RSN uses, beginning with Introduction to Embroidery. The RSN's Certificate and Diploma in Technical Hand Embroidery offers students the opportunity to learn a range of techniques to a very high technical standard. The Future Tutors course is specifically designed for those pursuing a career in teaching technical hand embroidery. The RSN's BA (Hons) Degree course is the only UK degree course solely focussed on hand embroidery and offers students opportunities to learn core stitch techniques, which they are then encouraged to apply in contemporary and conceptual directions. Graduates can go on to find careers in embroidery relating to fashion, couture and costume; to interiors and soft furnishings or in the area of textile art including jewellery and millinery.

At its Hampton Court headquarters, the RSN welcomes people for all kind of events from private lessons to bespoke stitching holidays, intensive Certificate and Diploma studies, tours around our exhibitions, which comprise either pieces from our own textile collections or students' work, or study days looking at particular pieces or techniques from our Collection. Work by students and from the Collection also forms the core of a series of lectures and presentations available to those who cannot get to the RSN. The RSN now offers a series of Distance Learning courses for people who cannot attend their classes, across many of the most familiar techniques.

The RSN Collection of textiles comprises more than 2,000 pieces, all of which have been donated, because as a charity the RSN cannot afford to purchase additions. The pieces were given so that they would have a home for the future and to be used as a resource for students and researchers. The Collection comes from all over the world, illustrating many different techniques and approaches to stitch and embellishment.

The RSN Studio undertakes new commissions and conservation work for many different clients, including public institutions, places of worship, stately homes and private individuals, again illustrating the wide variety of roles embroidery can play, from altar frontals and vestments for churches to curtains, hangings and chair covers for homes and embroidered pictures as works of art.

Over the last few years the RSN has worked with a number of prestigious names including Sarah Burton OBE for Alexander McQueen, Vivienne Westwood's Studio for Red Carpet Green Dress, Patrick Grant's E Tautz, the late L'Wren Scott, Nicholas Oakwell Couture for the GREAT Britain Exhibition, the Jane Austen House Museum, Liberty London, the V&A Museum of Childhood and M&S and Oxfam for Shwopping.

Most recently, the RSN created a den for HRH The Duchess of Cambridge's garden at the RHS Hampton Court Garden Festival and a portrait of the RSN Patron, HRH The Duchess of Cornwall, in Blackwork technique.

For more information about the RSN, its courses, studio, shop and exhibitions, see www.royal-needlework.org.uk, and for its degree programme see www.rsndegree.uk.

Hampton Court Palace, Surrey, home of
the Royal School of Needlework

INTRODUCTION TO EMBROIDERED BOXES

Ever since I was a little girl, I have been fascinated with small boxes in a variety of shapes, sizes and materials. I used to love going to car boot sales and other second-hand markets with my mother so that I could add to my collection. The boxes I collected were a range of shapes and sizes – round, square, rectangular, hexagonal; both large and small.

My love of boxes continued into adulthood. As an apprentice at the Royal School of Needlework, I was taught to make my own fabric-covered boxes, starting with a simple 5cm (2in) cubed box, before progressing to a more creative embroidered box to my own original design and specifications.

The focus of this book will be on hand-embroidery techniques, but you can add machine embroidery to your boxes as well. Use the art of box-making as a way to showcase your embroidery, as an alternative to mounting or framing your work. It is possible to use any embroidery technique to embellish your box – appliqué, surface stitching, silk shading and stumpwork, as well as adding beads or jewels. The resultant boxes make ideal gifts to give to loved ones.

This book covers the construction of a basic box, along with instructions on framing up your fabric ready for embroidery, information on materials and details of my chosen embroidery stitches. I also guide you fully through three projects that cover different aspects of embroidered box construction, such as different cutting techniques, and applying fastenings and hinges. For each project I have tried to use fabrics and threads that are readily available, but if these cannot be sourced easily, alternatives can be substituted, often with equally pleasing results.

Box-making requires great precision and accuracy; once you master these skills, there are no limits to the boxes you can create.

I hope that this book inspires you to enjoy box-making as much as I do, and to help you to develop your skills and knowledge so that you can create your own keepsake embroidered boxes.

8

Rainbow stacking boxes

These seven boxes stack neatly into one another. The boxes are sized in increments of 1.2cm (½in), the largest being 11.2cm³ (4⁷⁄₁₆in³). A simple rainbow, worked in rows of stem stitch, has been embroidered on the front of each box.

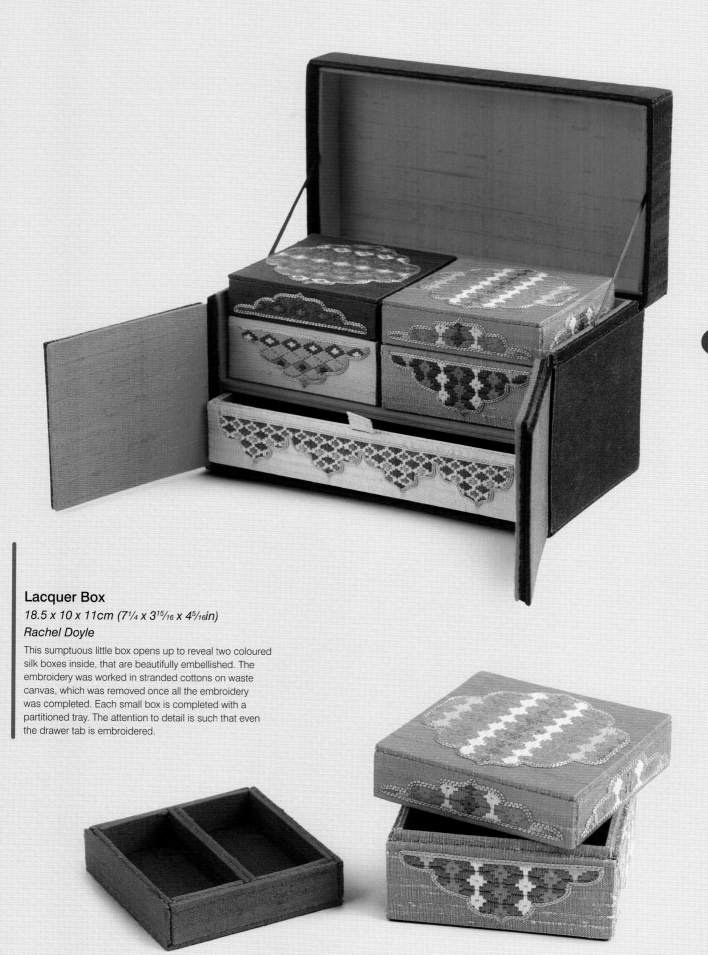

Lacquer Box

18.5 x 10 x 11cm (7¼ x 3¹⁵⁄₁₆ x 4⁵⁄₁₆in)

Rachel Doyle

This sumptuous little box opens up to reveal two coloured silk boxes inside, that are beautifully embellished. The embroidery was worked in stranded cottons on waste canvas, which was removed once all the embroidery was completed. Each small box is completed with a partitioned tray. The attention to detail is such that even the drawer tab is embroidered.

THE HISTORY OF EMBROIDERED BOXES

Across the centuries, wonderful boxes have been made from a variety of materials including wood, metal, ivory and bone.

Reliquaries – containers of religious objects – became an important part of Christian practice from around the fourth century. The earliest reliquaries were crafted using gold, silver or enamel, and were intended to contain relics such as a saint's bones or fragments of cloth from a saint's vestments. These boxes were vital assets for churches and abbeys, and were often used as a point of focus during prayers. Later, when there was little or no proof of their historic authenticity, many reliquaries were melted down or pulled apart in order to recover precious metals and gems.

A popular form of embroidery during the seventeenth century was raised embroidery. It flourished between 1640 and 1680, during the reigns of Charles I and Charles II. Embroidery at this time was used to embellish pictures, mirror frames and caskets. Highly decorative embroidered caskets were made and used by girls in the seventeenth century. Women made sure that their daughters were studious in their needlework training so as to inherit as many skills and stitches as they themselves knew. Having learned the basic techniques and applied embroidery stitches to a sampler, the girls – as young as six or seven years old – would progress to embroidering needlework pictures, small cabinets or panels of beadwork. Wealthy households would employ a resident tutor to supervise the girls' needlework.

Embroidered caskets of the seventeenth century were used to hold a variety of objects. Some were designed as writing cabinets to contain paper and inkwells; others held jewellery, brooches or perfume bottles. Some were used solely to keep needlework tools and threads. The actual style of the cabinets varied: early examples were simply rectangular boxes with plain lids.

Later the caskets became more complex, including numerous sections and compartments; some featured doors that opened to reveal a set of drawers, often with secret compartments behind, to hide away treasures.

The lids of these more complicated caskets had sloping sides, which could hold a mirror. They also included trays that lifted out to reveal a space for storing larger items. These complex caskets were fastened with locks and handles, and feet were also attached. The caskets were usually lined with pink or red silk.

Victorian Box
32 x 23 x 12cm (12⅝ x 9¹/₁₆ x 4¾in)

From the personal collection of Margaret Dier

This box features details in silk ribbon embroidery using ombre ribbons to form the roses.

The majority of the designs for these caskets would have been drawn onto fabric by professional pattern drawers, using the pattern books of the day. They would include numerous figures, flowers, leaves, animals and birds, with no regard for scale – all jostling for position.

Many caskets were in raised work, better known as stumpwork, which is a term that first came into use in the nineteenth century. A seventeenth-century casket could easily comprise twenty-five or more separate pieces of embroidery. The embroidery was worked on linen or silk in separate panels for the top, sides and edgings of the lid. Some of the embroidery was worked directly onto the fabric, but much was worked separately and applied later – these were known as 'slips'. A great variety of threads was used: metal threads, silk threads of various weights and textures, and crewel wool; the panels were often also embellished with beads and spangles, and bordered with braid. Occasionally the caskets would include the initials of the embroiderer. When the embroidered panels were complete, they were sent away to a cabinet maker, who mounted and fitted them to the chosen shape of the box. The boxes themselves were often fitted with compartments for sewing and writing implements, often with a mirror inside. Many caskets had secret compartments.

The subjects chosen to decorate these cabinets were often biblical as the Bible was central to seventeenth-century life. One famous example is a casket embroidered by Martha Edlin (1660–1725), whose work can be seen in the Victoria & Albert Museum in London. Edlin was a prolific and talented embroiderer. Her education in needlework resulted in the creation of a coloured sampler and a whitework sampler, and she completed her embroidered casket in 1671, aged only eleven years. Around the sides of the box are panels showing scenes from the Old Testament, such as the Seven Virtues with Justice and the Elements.

Many caskets are now on display in museums and stately homes where they can be seen and appreciated by the public. Some caskets have retained the vivid colours of their embroideries as they have been stored in protective cases.

Today, embroidered boxes are usually made using fabric-covered card; and the maker will interline the box themselves, rather than sending it to a cabinet-maker for completion.

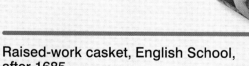

Raised-work casket, English School, after 1685

34 x 28 x 16cm (13⅜ x 11 x 6⁵⁄₁₆in)

Satin weave silk in silk thread, metal thread, wax, mica, parchment, pearls, metal purl and bullion, straw, glass beads, silk cord, linen ribbon and padding. Stitches include French knots, detached buttonhole and metal work. (Dorset County Museum, 1955.2.9)

MATERIALS AND TOOLS

FABRICS

For the boxes in this book I have used a variety of fabrics to demonstrate the different effects that can be achieved. The weight of the fabric is very important: it should not be too heavy, nor too light. Always buy the best quality of fabric available, to ensure that your embroidered box will last for many years.

The fabrics listed here will give you the best results.

Quilting cotton Quilting cotton gives excellent results. I recommend using a quilting cotton fabric on your first box. Patterned fabrics add more interest to your boxes; however, these need to be chosen with care. Fabrics with smaller patterns generally work better than those with larger patterns.

Silk There are different types available, which vary in weight. I prefer to use a smooth medium-weight silk such as a dupion. Silk can often have 'slubs', which are slight irregularities in the fibres. Take care that the grain of the silk always runs in the same direction. Any silk panels to be embroidered will need to be backed with a cotton fabric first.

Lawn Lawn is a very fine cotton fabric. It has a fine, high-count weave which results in a silky feel. It is available in a wide range of patterns and colours.

Linen With a smooth texture and distinctive slub, linen is a good choice for use on embroidered boxes. Linen is usually available in natural colours. It is available in an even weave for counted thread embroidery, as well as a weave more suited for free embroidery.

Calico Calico is a very useful cotton fabric for backing other fabrics before you embroider onto them. Use a bleached calico if you are backing white or pale fabrics; otherwise, a medium-weight natural calico will prove suitable for most embroidered box projects.

Avoid covering your box using fabrics with stripes until you are more experienced in box-making. Avoid using furnishing fabrics as well, as these are too thick to cover a box, and will result in your box not fitting together properly.

PADDING

Some boxes benefit from having additional padding. The amount of padding used depends on what the box will be used for. If the box has additional embroidery it can be advantageous to use padding underneath the embroidered panels to cushion any ends taken through to the back.

As a general rule, I do not use padding on the outside of the box, as it will not look as crisp and sharp, with the exception of the lid, which benefits from additional padding.

Felt padding Use a good-quality felt in white or a matching colour to the fabric being used, to pad your box (see pages 62–63).

Wadding (batting) Quilters' wadding will add extra loft or thickness to your boxes, but will not be as smooth as felt padding.

Carpet felt padding A good-quality carpet felt can be used to add more height to your box. It will need to be stitched to calico in a frame first before it is used to cover the card.

Opposite:

A selection of different fabrics suitable for box construction and covering.

EMBROIDERY THREAD

There is a wide range of embroidery threads available, and many come in different weights and colours. The most widely used threads are those made from natural fibres such as cotton, wool or silk.

Some threads can be separated and mixed with other threads in the same needle, other threads are twisted and cannot be divided. I suggest that you experiment with the threads listed below to find out if they achieve a good result.

Stranded cotton A widely used thread that is made up of six strands twisted together that can be separated before stitching (see page 38). It is a slightly shiny thread that is available in 8m (26¼ft) skeins.

Crewel wool A fine two-ply worsted yarn that is available in a wide range of subtle colours, crewel wool is used for free embroidery as well as canvaswork. Several strands can be used together in the needle to make a thicker thread. It is available in skeins of 25m (82ft).

Cotton perlé A tightly twisted thread with a lustrous finish, cotton perlé can be worked in the needle without separating the strands. It is available in a range of sizes and colours.

Silk threads Silk threads give a lovely shine to your embroidery but can be a little more challenging to work with. There are a wide variety of silk threads available. Some silk threads are used in the same way as stranded cotton.

Silk threads are not readily available on the high street so it is best to look for them online.

Metallic threads The technique of using metal threads is known as goldwork. There is a wide range of threads that generally fall into two categories: metal threads that you stitch down with a fine thread, known as couching, and metal threads or purls that are like coils of wire that you cut up and stitch down like beads.

These threads are available from specialist suppliers.

Silk ribbons Silk ribbons add an extra quality to your embroidery. They are available in widths of 2mm (1/16in), 4mm (3/16in), 7mm (1/4in) and 13mm (1/2in). I usually work with 4mm (3/16in) silk ribbon. Silk ribbons come in a variety of colours, both plain and variegated.

SEWING THREAD

Sewing threads are readily available in an extensive range of colours on reels that hold 100m (110yd) lengths. A polyester sewing thread is preferable to a cotton thread as it is less likely to snap.

A matching thread is essential to box-making; I prefer one in a shade that is ever so slightly darker than the fabric, as it is less likely to show.

BUTTONHOLE THREAD

This is an extra strong thread used for framing up and mounting. It is available in reels of 30m (98½ft). I like to use a buttonhole thread for lacing fabric over card (see pages 66–68) as it is much stronger than a sewing thread.

A selection of embellishments including Swarovski crystals, flat-backed crystals, sequins, buttons, bugle beads, seed beads and ribbons.

EMBELLISHMENTS

Embellishments are a way of adding decoration to the surface of the fabric. These can be jewels, beads or buttons, or fastenings.

There are a number of embellishments or decorations that can be added to your boxes to enhance them and add a little sparkle. It is a great opportunity to use your stash of beads, buttons, sequins and jewels.

Beading This term is used to describe attaching beads to fabric. Beads can be stitched individually or in groups, depending on your design. It is advisable to use a matching thread; run your thread through some beeswax first to strengthen it. Beading thread is also available, which is very strong and made for this purpose. Use a fine needle to securely stitch the beads to the fabric.

Jewels There is a good variety of jewels and gemstones available, which vary in size, shape and price.

Some crystals have holes which can be used to stitch the gems to the fabric. Use an invisible thread in a fine needle to attach the crystals to the fabric.

Other crystals are flat-backed and can be fixed to fabric using adhesive. These jewels are either 'hot-fix' jewels that are attached to the fabric using heat, or 'cold-fix' jewels that are attached to the fabric using a specialist glue. Always test these first on a piece of scrap fabric and follow the manufacturers' instructions carefully.

Ribbons Double satin-backed, petersham or silk ribbons can be used as embellishments. Use ribbons or cords as 'tabs' on trays. Ribbons can also be used as 'stays' inside the box to prevent the lid from opening too far (see pages 151 and 153).

FASTENINGS

It is important to consider all fastenings carefully. Having the right fastening can really enhance the look of your finished box. Wherever possible, I prefer to stitch any fastenings in place rather than glue them down.

Jewellery box fastenings Spend time sourcing the right fastening, so that it complements your hand-embroidered box. A wide variety of fastenings are available, including clasps, latches and even locks and keys. Take care to consider any fastenings carefully to ensure that they fit within your box.

Hinges These are available in a variety of sizes in either brass or silver colour. Metal hinges make an alternative to a fabric hinge. Attach them securely to your box.

Covered buttons A button made from a matching fabric can add a professional quality to your box. Buttons in a variety of sizes are available from most haberdashery shops or departments, and you can cover these yourself (see page 75). Most fabrics work well, but fine fabrics will benefit from additional interfacing on the back.

Knobs and feet Drawer handles or knobs are widely available and can be screwed into the box panel; alternatively, make sure that any fastenings are attached securely. Take care to use ones that are the correct proportions for your box.

Metal studs or brass feet are made with split pins for fixing them to your box (see page 144). These are easily available online. Alternatively, you could make your own feet from fabric-covered card (see page 156 for an example).

EMBROIDERY EQUIPMENT

Embroidery scissors Sharp scissors are essential for every embroiderer. You will need one pair of scissors to cut threads and a separate pair to cut through metal threads.

Baby brush Use a soft brush to brush away any excess pounce after transferring your design to fabric (see page 37).

Fabric shears A large pair of sharp scissors is essential for cutting fabrics. Treat them with respect and they will last for years.

Thimbles Useful for working through several layers of padding or stitching through leather.

Acid-free tissue paper I always like to work on acid-free tissue paper; this helps to protect your embroidery from getting dirty while working.

Screwdriver A small flathead screwdriver is very useful for tightening the screw on your hoop frame, to ensure that your fabric is kept as taut as possible.

Pricking tool This tool holds a fine needle that is used to make a series of small holes through a piece of tracing paper to mark the outline of a design – known as a 'pricking'.

Black fineline pen Use a fine black pen to draw out your designs. Use a very fine waterproof pen to draw your design carefully on your fabric.

Artist's paintbrush Use a very fine paintbrush to transfer your design to the fabric and a larger brush to create a painted background for your embroidery.

Watercolour paints Use watercolour paint to transfer your design onto fabric and to add a wash of colour to your background fabric.

Tweezers Fine pointed tweezers are used to remove unwanted threads from your work or used to help manipulate threads.

Cotton string Use good-quality string to lace around the arms of your slate frame to achieve a good tension.

Webbing Cotton herringbone tape is securely stitched to the sides of your fabric in the slate frame.

Glass-headed pins Glass-headed pins are easy to use and are kind on fingers when pushed through fabric into card.

Bracing needle A very large curved needle with a large eye, it is used to lace string through the webbing and around the arms on a slate frame. It is also known as a curved spring needle.

Pounce (not shown) Pounce is used to rub through the pricking to transfer the design temporarily to your fabric. It is made from ground charcoal (black) and ground cuttlefish (white). A mid-tone grey can be made by blending the two together.

Stiletto This small tool with a tapered point is used to make holes in fabric without breaking the threads. Stilettos can be made from metal, wood or plastic.

Mellor This flat, pointed tool is useful when working with metal threads; it can also be used to neaten and tidy up laced threads – see page 140.

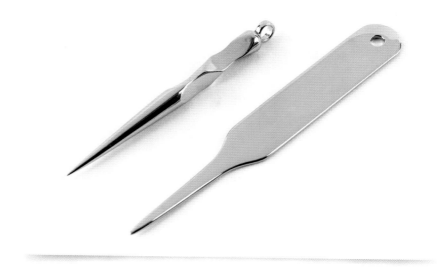

NEEDLES

Curved needle These are essential in box-making; I like to use a fine, sharp quilter's curved needle. Curved beading needles are also useful but are very fine and thus prone to breaking easily.

Embroidery needles I use a wide variety of different embroidery needles – the size is determined by the size of the thread and fabric being handled.

The three types of needle used for embroidery have longer eyes than those used for sewing.

Embroidery or **crewel needles** are medium length with a sharp point. They are used for fine and medium-weight embroidery on fabric.

Chenille needles are similar to embroidery needles but are longer and thicker. The eyes are larger to accommodate thicker threads. Chenille needles are useful for plunging metal threads through to the back of your work. They are also ideal for ribbon embroidery.

Tapestry needles are almost the same as chenille needles, except that they have a blunt point. Tapestry needles are used for canvaswork and embroidery on evenweave fabric.

FRAMES

A good-quality slate frame is essential for working a larger piece of embroidery or for working several box panels at the same time. Your fabric is stitched onto the rollers of the slate frame, before the arms are positioned, and held in place with split pins. Lace the sides of the fabric to the frame with string. It can take a while to frame up, but it is worth the effort due to the tight tension that can be achieved. I usually work on a 60cm (24in) slate frame, but other sizes are available.

HOOP FRAMES

Hoop or ring frames are available in various sizes. They consist of two circular sections, one of which fits neatly inside the other, holding the fabric firmly in between. I like to work all my embroidery in a hoop or slate frame, to keep the fabric tight and prevent wrinkles in my work. Choose one suitable for the size of your project. I suggest you use one that attaches to a seat frame or table clamp to keep your hands free while working.

CONSTRUCTION TOOLS

Mountboard I like to use an acid-free mountboard that is 1.5mm (¹⁄₁₆in) thick. Mountboard is available in sheets of A1 size – 84.1 x 59.1cm (33⅛ x 23¼in).

Cutting mat A self-healing cutting mat is essential when cutting out mountboard, so as not to damage your work surface. Buy a good-quality one. A3 – 42 x 29.7cm (16½ x 11¾in) – is a good size to start with.

Knife I use a utility knife with a retractable blade but you could choose to use a craft knife. Always ensure that the blade is sharp and change the blade regularly.

Metal ruler This is essential when cutting mountboard. I prefer to use a safety ruler with a ridge that protects my fingers.

Plastic ruler Use a clear plastic ruler to measure out your card pieces – one that includes a grid pattern is very useful.

Double-sided tape Use a good-quality double-sided tape. 12mm (½in) is an ideal width.

Set square To ensure 90-degree corners, always use a set square. I use a clear plastic ruler with lines at 90 degrees, to ensure that all pieces are square.

Mount cutter A good-quality mount cutter is essential if you wish to make a box with more than four sides. These are usually purchased with a metal ruler onto which the blade clips.

Paper scissors Use a pair of paper scissors purely for cutting double-sided tape, so that you do not mess up your embroidery or fabric scissors.

Pencil I prefer to use a mechanical pencil as it stays sharp. The finer the better – I advise that you use 0.3mm or 0.5mm.

Pair of compasses Use a pair of compasses and a sharp pencil to draw an accurate circle.

Compass cutter A compass or circle cutter is a useful tool for cutting circles; ensure that the blade is sharp for absolute accuracy.

BASIC TECHNIQUES

DESIGNING YOUR BOX

When designing a box, it is important to think about what the box will be used for. There is inspiration all around – there are boxes of varying shapes and sizes everywhere, from buildings, postboxes and grandfather clocks to the packaging we see in shops, such as shoe boxes, cake boxes and chocolate boxes.

The purpose of your own embroidered box could be to hold everyday items, such as jewellery, sewing equipment, or pencils and pens – or it could be a chest of drawers that holds many different items.

BEFORE YOU BEGIN:

Ask yourself these questions before you begin to design, to help you decide upon the purpose of your box:

- Will the box be a gift?
- What will the box contain?
- How will the box open – will the box have doors or a drawer?
- What type of fastenings do I wish to include?
- Will there be anything inside the box – will the box have a tray or compartments?
- What fabrics do I want to use?
- How will the box be embellished?
- Do I have an existing piece of embroidery that can be used on the box?
- How many box panels will be embroidered?
- Will the embroidery continue around the sides of the box?

CONSIDERATIONS

As a starting point for your box, your fabric choice needs careful thought. An embroidered box is an opportunity for you to use fabric from your existing stash, if chosen wisely. Consider how much wear and tear the box will withstand. A box for everyday use – such as a pencil box – would be better made from a sturdy fabric such as cotton or linen.

Plain fabrics are the simplest to use as there is only the textural quality to consider. Patterned fabrics can be used, though keep in mind that a smaller pattern generally works better. Combining patterned and plain fabrics can work very effectively; however, striped fabrics need to be chosen with care, and are only suitable for more experienced box-makers, as the stripes need to be matched around all sides of the box.

The weight of the fabric is also important. A heavy fabric such as velvet or denim is not suitable as your box will not fit together correctly. The weight of the fabric must also be right for the size of the box – a tiny box made of a heavy material will look clumsy.

The design of some boxes is enhanced with the addition of fastenings, a lid, or feet that raise the box off the surface. Think about the type of lid carefully: there are several to consider. Will it be a pop-on lid, a hinged lid, an overlapping lid, or a lid that sits flush with the sides of the box? All options need to be studied before you complete the design of your box – see page 74 for some ideas. In terms of feet and fastenings, source these additions carefully to ensure that they complement your design.

While there are plenty of practical considerations to bear in mind, I do encourage you to set free your creative side and, most of all, have fun with box-making.

Opposite:
The design for the *Afternoon Tea Box* (pages 92–115) was inspired by a visit to Claridge's hotel in London.

PLANNING YOUR BOX

Once you have come up with an idea, I encourage you to think about your design for a while and make a prototype before you get started.

The size of your box will need to suit its purpose, so the proportions will need to be considered carefully to achieve the right look for your project. A small box can be a little fiddly to construct and a larger box is not easy to handle.

MAKING A PROTOTYPE

Once you have decided on your box design, it is a worthwhile exercise to construct a prototype from cereal box card or other scrap card to check you are happy with the size and shape before starting with the project. There is no need to cover the card prototype in fabric.

Make a prototype of the external box only – it is not necessary to construct the internal box, as the prototype simply enables you to check the proportions and overall size of the box. However, be sure to include any doors and lids in your prototype.

The prototype shown below is for the basic box, which is constructed on pages 60–73.

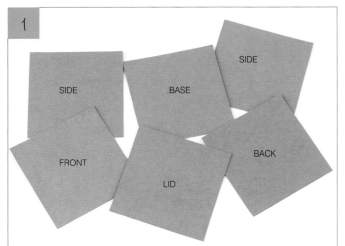

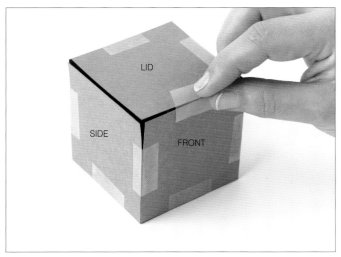

1 Measure and cut the pieces accurately according to the dimensions given above. Label each piece clearly.

2 Stick the pieces together with sticky tape. Check the prototype to ensure that your box is a neat fit with no uneven gaps.

WORKING OUT THE BOX MEASUREMENTS

It is important to carefully work out all the box measurements following the 2mm rule (see right). Clearly write down all the measurements you will need and double-check them all. While working out all the measurements, it is important to think about how the box will be constructed. Usually the base sits within the front, back and sides but if not, the measurements will need to be adjusted accordingly.

PLANNING THE INTERIOR BOX

Although you need only create a prototype for the exterior box, the interior needs equal thought and consideration. Have fun choosing different patterned fabrics for the inside to add an element of surprise to your project. The inside fabric can be a total contrast to the fabric that you use on the outside.

Think carefully about what the box will contain to allow enough space when divisions and compartments are in position. A sewing box will need to have enough space for threads, scissors, needles and a thimble, for example.

THE 2MM RULE

I have used metric measurements when designing and constructing the projects in this book – for the purposes of accuracy, I advise that you adhere to the metric measurements wherever possible to ensure the success of your own projects. If you are using imperial measurements the results may not be exactly the same – however, for the purposes of this book, in most instances the imperial measurement equivalent to 2mm is 1/16in.

Before beginning to construct a hand-stitched fabric box it is important to understand how the box is constructed and the measurements needed so that the box fits together accurately. When mountboard is covered with fabric it has a depth of 2mm. This measurement is used when calculating the measurements for the entire box.

Any lid will sit on top of the main box, so the height of the main box will need to be reduced by 2mm to allow for the lid.

The sides of the box fit within the front and back pieces, so the sides will need to be reduced by 2mm on each side, resulting in the sides being 4mm (3/16in) narrower in total.

If a thicker mountboard or fabric is used, the measurements will need to be adjusted accordingly.

Posture and lighting

Find a comfortable space to work in. If possible, clear everything away except for the tools and materials you need before you begin. Be sure you are working at a comfortable height – adjust your chair if possible. While stitching, the hours often fly by – remember to take regular breaks.

It is important to work in good lighting, I prefer to work during daylight hours; however, a lamp with a daylight bulb is a good substitute.

DESIGNING YOUR EMBROIDERY

Once you have decided what type of box you are making and worked out all the box measurements, you can design the embroidery that is going to embellish your box. It is worth thinking about how the box will be handled before designing the embroidery. It is not advisable to embroiderer onto areas that are handled excessively. The use of delicate embroidery – such as goldwork or stumpwork – should be considered carefully, as you will not want to damage the threads.

Designing a piece of embroidery for a three-dimensional item is very different from designing a piece that will be placed behind glass when complete. It comes with extra challenges. The design for the embroidery could begin with the fabric you are using: if your fabric has an interesting design, you may wish to use that as the basis for your embroidery.

Decide where on the box the embroidery is going to be placed – it does not have to be on the lid. The embroidery could continue onto the sides of the box.

1 Draw your embroidery design on paper within the box piece measurements to ensure that it fits the box piece it is intended for.

2 Once you have refined your design, trace over your design lines with a fine black waterproof pen.

3 Use this design to transfer your design to your fabric. Allow extra fabric around the edges for turnings.

When I have designed a piece of embroidery, I like to think about it for a little while to ensure that I am happy with it. If you have constructed a prototype, you can position your embroidery design over the prototype to get a real feel for how your box will look. I like to colour my design with coloured pencils too.

CHOOSING THE EMBROIDERY STITCHES

When you have designed your embroidery it is necessary to create a stitch plan. It is important to plan your embroidery at this stage as it is not always easy to adapt your design once the stitching has been started. I usually photocopy my outline drawing several times and use it to scribble ideas onto before making the stitch plan.

Decide what techniques you would like to use on each panel of your box and reconsider using any elaborate techniques or stitches that may get damaged during the handling of the box. Stitches can also look different from panel to panel, depending on the thread and scale you use, so experiment to find out.

If you are including fastenings, these also need to be considered carefully so that they complement any embroidery and embellishments on your box.

Below: the stitch plan for the side panels of the *Stumpwork Casket* (see pages 116–155).

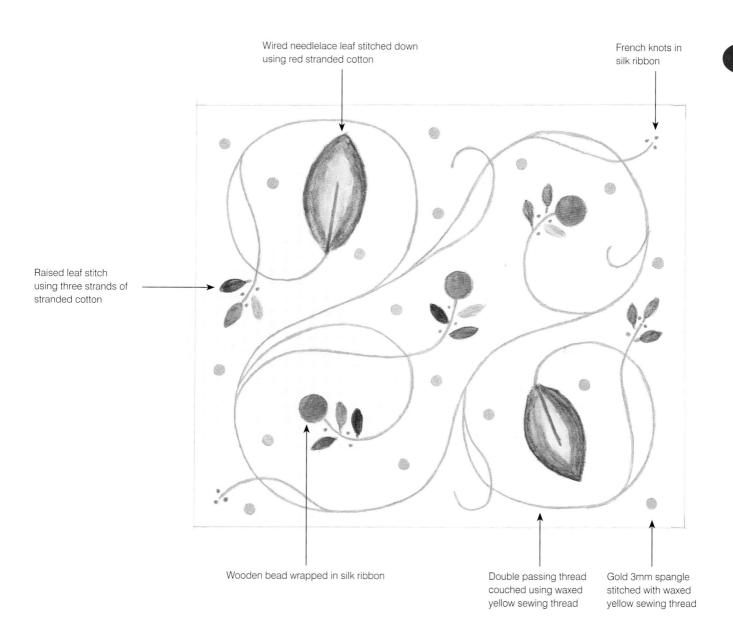

Wired needlelace leaf stitched down using red stranded cotton

French knots in silk ribbon

Raised leaf stitch using three strands of stranded cotton

Wooden bead wrapped in silk ribbon

Double passing thread couched using waxed yellow sewing thread

Gold 3mm spangle stitched with waxed yellow sewing thread

FRAMING UP A HOOP FRAME

A 'hands-free' hoop frame will make your embroidery much easier to handle, once you get accustomed to using it. The important thing to remember is that your fabric must be at a very firm tension.

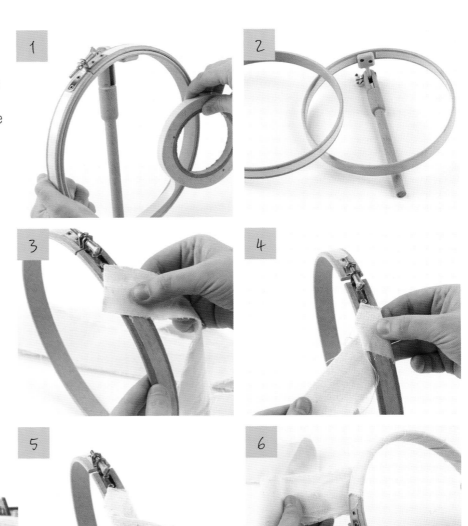

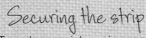

Securing the strip

To make your job easier, use a curved needle when securing the end of the fabric strip next to the frame's hard surface in step 3.

1 Attach a strip of double-sided sticky tape around the outside of the hoop frame, then repeat on the inside.

2 Separate the hoops.

3 Cut or tear a long strip of calico, 2.5–5cm (1–2in) wide. Peel off the backing from the double-sided sticky tape, then place one end of the calico strip on the sticky tape at an angle, starting at the screw of the outer frame.

4 Take the strip underneath to begin wrapping the hoop.

5 Wrap the strip around again, overlapping the previous edge as shown.

6 Continue wrapping all the way round the hoop.

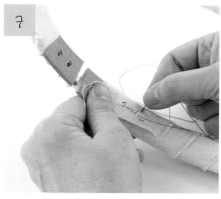

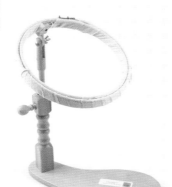

7 Trim away any excess calico, then secure the strip by oversewing half a dozen or so stitches at the end.

8 Repeat on the inner frame, then temporarily sit the smaller frame within the larger until you are ready to work. I recommend the use of a seat frame as shown here, which has a stem you can secure within a seat part, leaving your hands free to work. Floor stands and table clamps are also available to fit these kinds of hoops.

9 Unscrew the outer hoop to make it as large as possible, then cut your fabric to the size of your outer hoop, plus 5cm (2in) on every side.

10 Place the fabric over the inner hoop, then place the outer hoop over the top.

11 Gradually make the fabric taut, by alternately tightening the screw on the outer hoop (see 11b) and pulling the excess fabric outside of the hoop away from the centre. Pull evenly on all sides to avoid distorting the fabric.

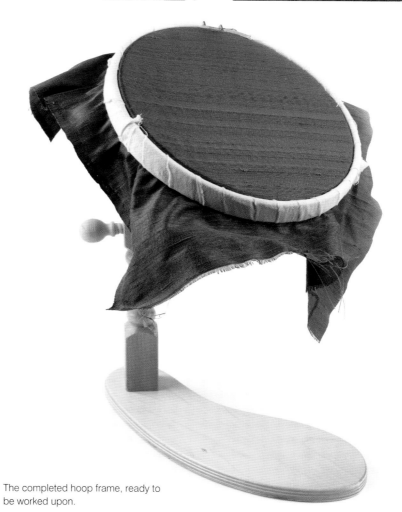

The completed hoop frame, ready to be worked upon.

FRAMING UP A SLATE FRAME

Here I will show you how to successfully frame up a slate frame. Once your fabric is secured to the calico (muslin) background, you can adjust the tension on the fabric by moving the frame's pins into different holes on the arms.

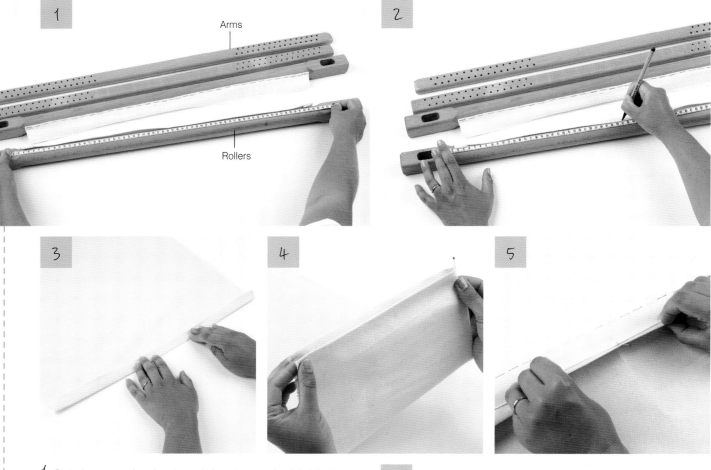

1 Slate frames are handmade, so it is not guaranteed that both rollers will be the same length. Check the length of both with a tape measure before you start. Measure the distance between the two large holes.

2 Mark each roller's mid-point on the webbing using a pencil.

3 Fold over the top and bottom of the calico (muslin) backing, on the grain of the fabric, by 1.5cm (⁹⁄₁₆in).

4 To find the centre of the fabric, fold it in half and insert a glass-headed pin at this point.

5 Match the glass-headed pin to the mid-point marked on the roller, and pin the calico (muslin) to the webbing so that the folded edge sits directly underneath the webbing.

6 Pin the folded calico (muslin) edge and webbing together. Do so by working outwards from the middle of the webbing to the right-hand edge, spacing the pins 2.5cm (1in) apart, smoothing the fabric at a slight tension against the webbing.

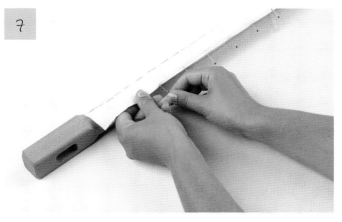

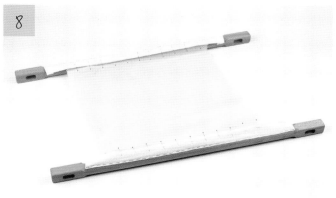

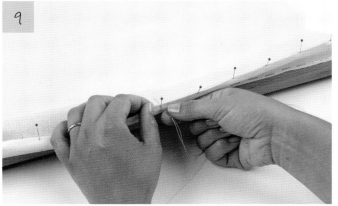

7 Return to the mid-point and then pin outwards to the left-hand edge, again spacing the pins about 2.5cm (1in) apart, attaching the calico (muslin) all the way along its length.

8 Repeat steps 4–7 on the opposite side of the roller so that each end of the calico (muslin) is pinned in place.

9 Thread a size 7 or 9 embroidery needle, or a large sharps needle, with buttonhole thread and tie a knot in the end. Starting at the mid-point, cast on the thread by making two overcast stitches, then continue the overcast stitches along towards the right-hand edge, locking both the calico (muslin) and webbing together.

10 The overcast stitches should be 3mm (⅛in) apart; alternate the lengths so that the tension is distributed evenly across the webbing. Varying the stitch size prevents the fabric ripping when the frame is tightened. Remove the glass-headed pins as you sew.

11 To finish off the thread at the edge of the calico (muslin), work several stitches overlapping those you have already done and then cut off the buttonhole thread.

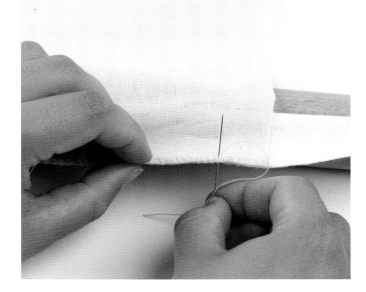

Cutting your background fabric
Make sure that you cut on the grain of the fabric so that the length and width are the same at both ends of the fabric. This will ensure an even tension to work on across your frame.

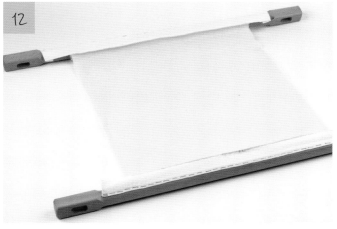

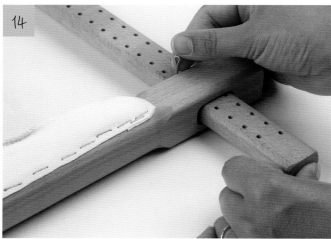

12 Return to the mid-point and sew outwards to the left-hand edge this time, using overcast stitch and buttonhole thread. Repeat steps 9–11 on the opposite roller; the calico (muslin) is now securely attached.

13 Slot the arms into the frame. Make sure that each arm is a mirror image of the other so that the holes in the arms are in the same place.

14 Insert the split pins or pegs into the holes to hold the rollers away from each other and to tighten the calico (muslin). The fabric should be tight but not drum-tight at this stage.

15 Pin a strip of cotton webbing, otherwise known as herringbone tape, to both unstitched edges of the calico (muslin) so that it sits evenly along the grain of the fabric. Two-thirds of the webbing should be on the fabric and the other third should be off the fabric.

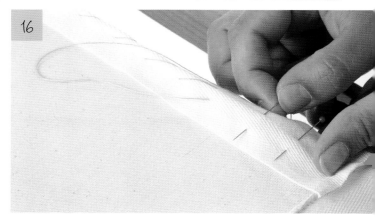

16 Thread a size 7–9 embroidery needle, or large sharps needle, with buttonhole thread and knot the end. Make two stitches through the calico (muslin) and webbing at the top of the frame, then cut off the knot. Work a diagonal stitch that is roughly 2cm (¾in) long through the webbing and up under the edge of the calico (muslin), pulling it firm as you go so that the webbing folds over the edge of the calico (muslin). When you reach the other end of the frame, cast off the buttonhole thread with two additional stitches. Repeat this process on the other side of the calico (muslin) so that both pieces of webbing are attached.

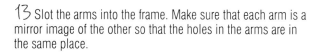

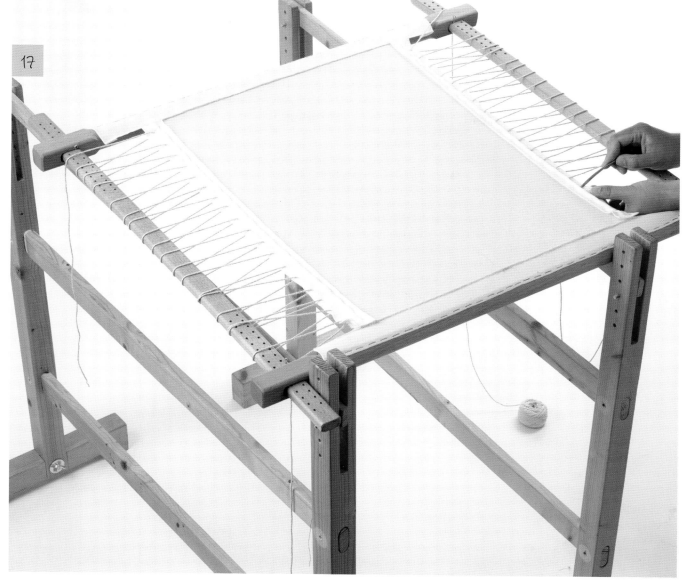

17 With your fabric secured, place the frame onto a trestle so that you can string it. Thread the end of a ball of string into an upholstery bracing needle. Starting at the top of one edge, take the needle down into the edge of the webbing – being careful not to insert it through the calico (muslin). Create stitches by coming up around the arm of the frame with the string every 2.5cm (1in). Once completed, cut the string leaving a 50cm (19¾in) tail on each end. Repeat this process on the other side of the frame.

18 Slacken off the frame by taking the split pins out of the arms and placing them in holes further towards the middle of the frame. Take your background fabric – here I have used purple silk – and lay this onto the calico (muslin) so that it sits in the same direction with the grains of both fabrics matching.

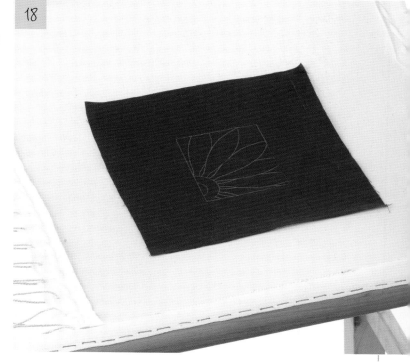

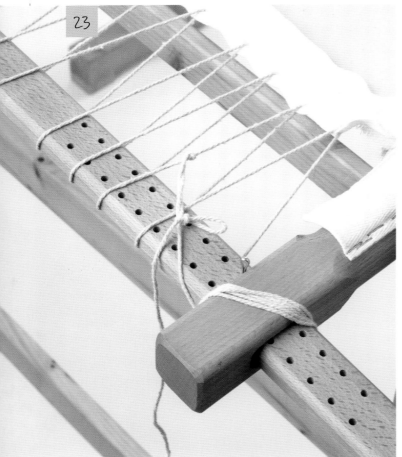

19 Place a pin through both layers of fabric, in the middle of each side, first pinning one side, then the opposite side, then repeating for the remaining two sides.

20 Continue placing pins roughly 2.5cm (1in) apart, working from the middle out, pinning one side in place and then turning the fabric around to ease the opposite side out.

21 Thread a needle with a doubled length of machine thread. Cast on at the edge of the calico (muslin) with a knot and two waste stitches, then cut the knot off. Scoop the needle through the purple silk for the first part of the herringbone stitch, then return to the calico (muslin) for the next stitch.

22 Continue to work this stitch around all four edges of the purple silk fabric. Remove the pins once the fabric is stitched.

23 Apply some more tension to the frame by moving the split pins further out from the middle of the frame; move them one by one, to increase the tension evenly.

Pinning out fabric

Both fabrics should lie flat and at the same tension. If puckers form in the fabric you are applying, you are pinning too tightly against the calico (muslin)

24 You now need to tighten the tension on the string. Starting from the centre of the right-hand strip of webbing, work towards one edge, pulling the string tight and adjusting all the loops. Secure the string with a slip knot at one end and then return to the middle of the webbing and work back in the opposite direction. You are aiming for the webbing edge to sit perpendicular to the arm of the frame so that the calico (muslin) is evenly stretched. Once one side of the frame is tensioned, tighten the opposite side using the same method.

25 To tension the frame so that it is drum-tight, stand the base of the frame upright on the floor and use the sole of your foot to push down the end of the bottom roller so that the split pin can be pulled out. Push down again to move the pin into a lower hole so that the tension on the fabric is increased. Repeat on the opposite side so that both split pins sit within the same corresponding holes, to give even tension across the frame. To doublecheck that the frame is at a consistent tension, measure the distance between the rollers at each side of the frame.

Take the pressure off

When tightening the string (as in step 24), pull the string against the arm part of the frame, as this takes pressure off your hands.

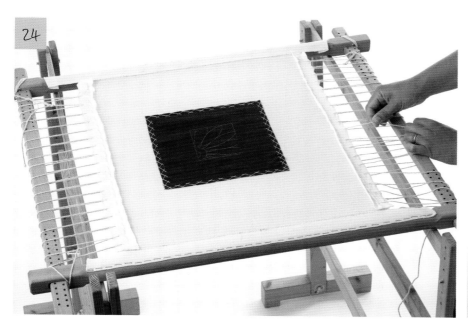

The framed-up fabric.

Keeping work clean

Once your fabric is framed, use either tissue paper or a piece of clean bed linen to protect your work.

TRANSFERRING A DESIGN

Even the most abstract, contemporary piece of embroidery benefits from some sort of design outline on the base fabric. The design lines will need to be completely hidden by stitch at some point during the construction, so the rules of thumb are to be very precise and steady in all your line drawing and to transfer only what you need; small fiddly dots and flourishes are better worked freehand in stitch.

TRACING

The simplest method is to trace your design from paper to fabric.

1 Work the design on paper fairly strongly, using a black pen. Lay the fabric flat over the paper, and make sure that you can see the design in the centre of the fabric, and square with the grain (if present).

2 Use a hard, sharp pencil – such as a 3H or 4H – to trace the design carefully onto the fabric. Use fine lines that are just visible – there is no need to work too darkly or strongly, as this makes it harder to hide the lines under your stitching later.

3 Make sure that you transfer every element of the design to the fabric; you may find it helpful to compare the paper original to the fabric before you move on.

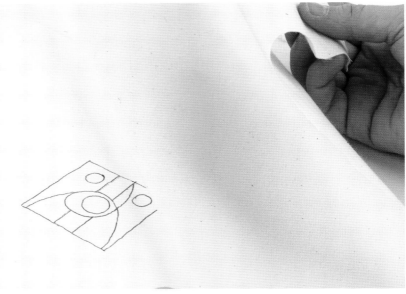

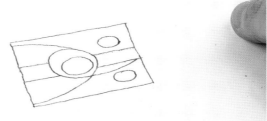

Thick material

To see the design through thicker material, you may need to draw out the design on tracing paper and to use a light source behind the design (such as a lightbox or simply a window).

THE PRICK AND POUNCE METHOD

Sometimes your fabric will be too thick or too textured to be able to use the tracing method for transferring your design; in these instances, the prick and pounce method is your best option.

1 Place your tracing on some padding such as thick felt or a folded piece of fabric. Insert a needle into a pricker and pierce the tracing paper along the design lines at 5mm (¼in) intervals.

2 Secure the pricking in position on your backing fabric with pins. Dab one end of a felt pad into the pounce, then rub the felt pad over the holes in the pricking in small circular motions.

3 Carefully remove the pins and lift the pricking away, ensuring that you do not spill any excess pounce. Pull the pins away vertically to avoid flicking the paper.

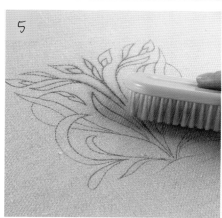

4 Before the pounce blows off the linen or becomes smudged, make the design outline permanent by painting over it with a small paintbrush and grey watercolour paint.

5 Once the paint has dried, remove any excess pounce by brushing it away with a soft brush.

SEPARATING STRANDS OF THREAD

When working with stranded cotton or a stranded silk thread, it is necessary to separate the strands individually and place together the required number of threads. This helps to give the embroidery a neater appearance.

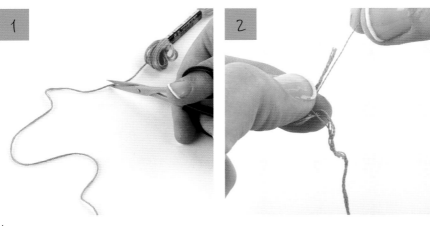

1 Cut a length of thread no longer than 30cm (12in).

2 Hold the thread at one end and gently pull out a single strand. Lay this on your work surface. Do not attempt to pull out more than a single strand or it will tangle.

3 Continue pulling out the strands individually, and place together the required number of strands.

Tip
Even when working with all six strands, it is necessary to separate all of them first. This helps to give the embroidery a smoother, more professional finish.

STARTING A THREAD

To achieve the best results, it is important to always start and finish your threads securely and neatly. The method shown here uses the **waste knot technique**, which ensures that the ends of the thread are neat and that you avoid having excess thread and knots on the back of your embroidery.

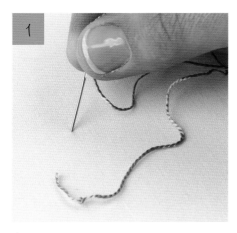

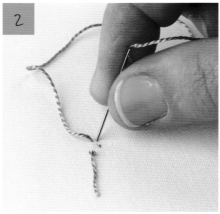

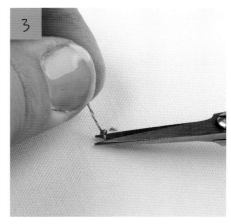

1 To start a thread, take a piece of thread no longer than 25cm (9¾in) and tie a knot in one end. Thread the needle and take the needle down through the fabric in an area that will be covered by stitching later.

2 Make two tiny stitches in the fabric to secure the thread.

3 Cut off the knot close to the fabric.

To finish the thread, make two tiny stitches in the fabric that will be covered by stitching and trim off the tail of thread. Alternatively, secure the thread on the back.

STARTING A SILK RIBBON

Silk ribbons are beautiful to work with; however, they are much thicker than normal embroidery thread. It is unusual to start the ribbons using the waste knot technique; instead, a small knot can be tied in the end of the ribbon and brought up from the back of the work. Alternatively, you can leave a tail of ribbon and secure the ribbon on the back of the fabric later, using a sewing thread.

Silk ribbons are very smooth – so much so that they frequently slip out of the eye of the needle. Attaching the ribbon to the needle (as shown below) will help prevent it from slipping out.

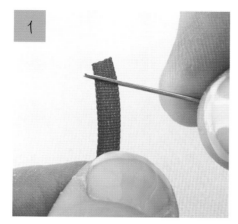

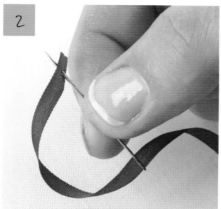

1 Thread a short length of silk ribbon onto a chenille needle.

2 Take the point of the needle through the ribbon near the end.

3 Pull through the point of the needle to secure the ribbon onto the needle. Tie a knot in the end.

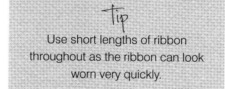

Tip
Use short lengths of ribbon throughout as the ribbon can look worn very quickly.

EMBROIDERY STITCHES

There is a great variety of embroidery stitches that can be combined and adapted to suit any box project, all of which can be achieved in almost any type of thread. Experiment with the different stitches and combine the techniques to add a personal touch to your work.

The stitches are divided into two main groups: surface stitches and raised stitches. I have included just a few stitches here. Don't be afraid to play with them all.

RUNNING STITCH

Running stitch is the most basic of all stitches and is quick and easy to work.

Start your thread on the design line. Pass the needle through the fabric at regular intervals. For a different result, leave wider spaces in between the stitches.

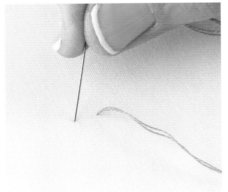

Running stitch can also be used to secure and gather fabric over a circular or semi-circular card piece (see page 90).

SPLIT STITCH

Split stitch was used extensively during the Middle Ages for embroidering the faces and hands of figures on ecclesiastical vestments.

Split stitch is used underneath satin stitch (see page 42) and around the outline of long and short stitch (see pages 44–45). It is a very useful stitch to raise the embroidery slightly and makes it easier for you to achieve a neat edge. It is essential to work this stitch in a soft thread such as stranded cotton or crewel wool, since each stitch is split. The stitching is similar in appearance to chain stitch.

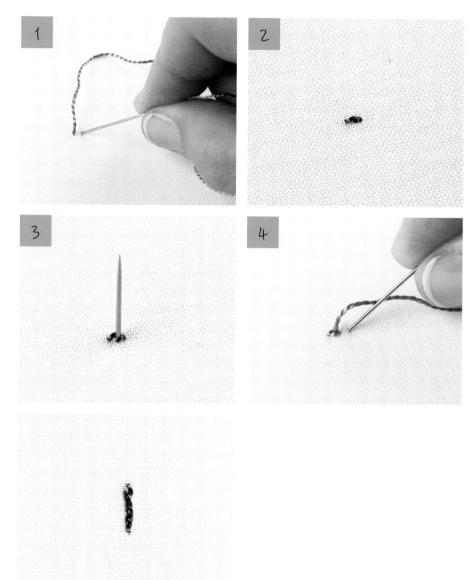

The completed stitch.

1 Start your thread within the design line and bring your needle out on the design line. To make your first stitch, take your needle down a little way along the line.

2 Pull the thread tight.

3 Bring your needle up in the centre of the previous stitch, splitting the thread. Pull the thread tight.

4 To complete the second stitch, take your needle down on the design line. Pull the thread tight. Keep the stitches small and an even size.

SATIN STITCH

This is a stitch that creates a smooth area of stitching. It can appear simple to work but practice is needed to ensure a neat and smooth appearance. Always work a small, tight split stitch around the edge before commencing with the satin stitch. The stitches can be worked in any direction. The effect is enhanced by working satin stitch in a lustrous thread such as stranded cotton or pure silk.

Start your thread within the shape that you are working. You may find it easier to draw on the stitch direction with a pencil first.

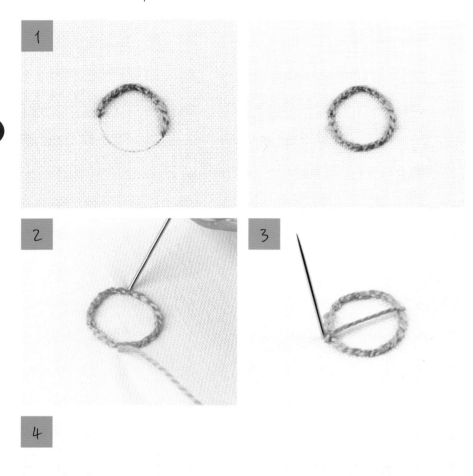

1 Stitch a small, tight split stitch around the edge, working the split stitch on the outer edge of your design line.

2 Bring your needle up outside the split stitch in the centre of the shape. Take your needle down on the other side, angling your needle inwards slightly.

3 Bring your needle up on the other side, close to the first stitch. Take care not to stitch through any of the split stitches.

4 Continue working across the shape to be filled. Work the stitches closely together so that they lie evenly.

The completed stitch.

STEM STITCH

Stem stitch is a very useful stitch that can be worked in individual rows or several rows worked close together, which can be shaded. It makes a neat twisted line that follows intricate curves well. It is similar to outline stitch, but the stitches run bottom-left to top-right along the stem. An even backstitch is formed on the back of the work.

Stem stitch can be successfully worked in any type of embroidery thread.

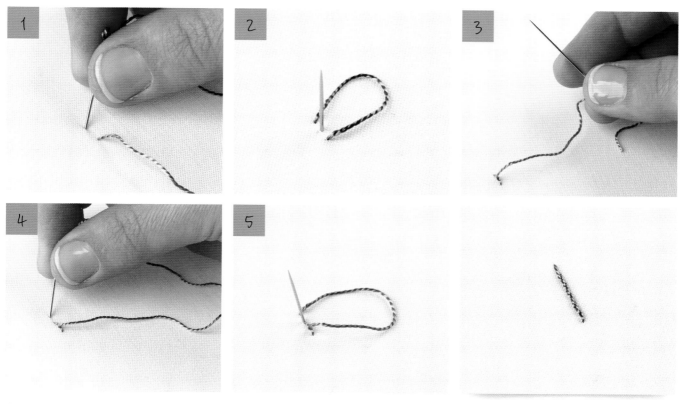

The completed stitch.

1 Start your thread on the design line, working towards you. Bring your needle out at the end of the line. Take your needle down on the design line, about 3mm (⅛in) away from where you started, pulling most of the thread through but leaving a loop to the right on the surface of the fabric.

2 Bring your needle up again on the design line, halfway back to the starting point.

3 Pull your thread through, tightening the first stitch.

4 Take your needle down again about 3mm (⅛in) away on the design line, leaving a loop on the surface of the fabric to the right.

5 Bring your needle up again on the design line, halfway back along the stitch, at the same point where the first stitch ended. Pull your thread tight.

Repeat the following steps along your design line, to complete a line of stem stitch.

LONG AND SHORT STITCH

Also known as silk shading, this technique is most successfully worked using a single strand of stranded cotton, but can also be worked using two strands.

When working a flower, first work the petal furthest back, then work forwards systematically in the order in which the petals overlap each other.

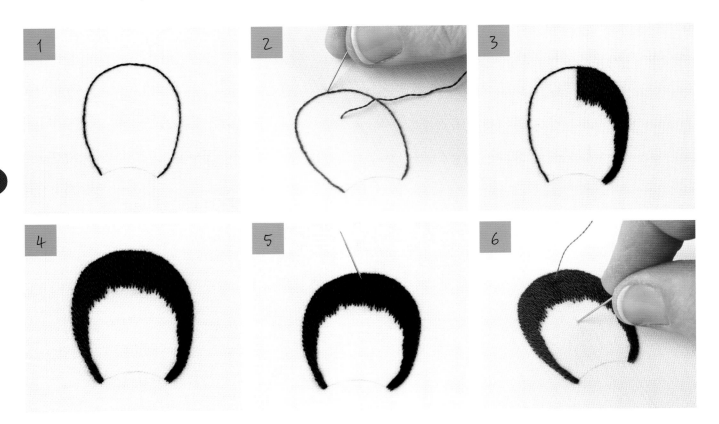

1 Any area of the design that is worked in long and short stitch must be prepared first by working split stitch around the outer edges of the shape (see page 41). It keeps the edges neat and raises the stitches slightly.

2 Start in the centre of the shape, bring your needle up within the split stitch edge. The first stitch, about 1cm (⅜in) in length, comes up within the petal and is taken down over the split stitch edge.

3 A stitch about two-thirds its length is laid next to it. This pattern of alternating long and short stitches is continued around the outer edge of the shape. Gradually swing the angle of the stitches to follow the shading directions. Vary the length of the stitches.

4 Complete the first row of alternating stitches.

5 Once the first row is complete, the second row is worked by bringing the needle up through the stitches of the first row, splitting the thread.

6 Take your needle down in the fabric to complete the first stitch of the second row. Continue along the row taking these stitches about a third of the way up into those of the first row. These stitches will be about the same length although varying them slightly will help to give a smoother shaded look.

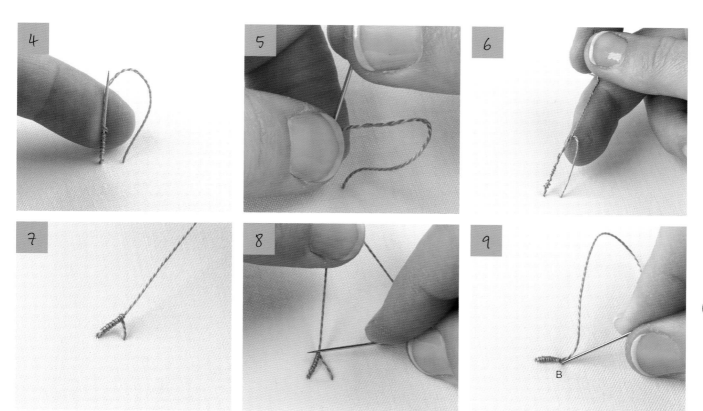

1 Bring your needle up at A, take your needle down at B, but do not pull the thread through.

2 Stab your needle up at A, but bring it only halfway through the fabric.

3 Holding the needle from below, twist the thread around the needle at A. The number of twists, when the thread is tightened, will eventually match the distance between A and B.

4 Hold the top of the needle and the threads firmly.

5 Hold onto the thread wraps, and draw the needle through, loosening the coil of threads slightly, to allow the needle to pass through freely.

6 Continue to pull the thread gently. Don't worry too much if the coils of thread appear a little loose at this stage.

The completed stitch.

7 Start to tighten the coils by pulling the thread.

8 Push the wraps down to the surface using the tip of your needle until the knot lies flat on the fabric. Take a little time to achieve a smooth knot.

9 Place the needle back into the fabric at the end of the coils at B and pull the thread through firmly.

COUCHING

Couching is used to attach a thread or group of threads to fabric at regular intervals, when they are too thick or too delicate to be stitched directly into the fabric. The word 'couching' comes from the French word, *coucher* (meaning, to lay down). Couching is often seen in metal thread embroidery but it can work very successfully with other threads. When couching metal threads, use a matching sewing thread to secure the metal thread to the fabric.

Start the sewing thread along the design line. If you are working with metal threads, it is advisable to run your sewing thread through some beeswax first, to give it extra strength.

For stitching down gold thread, I often use a polyester Gutermann thread 488 or 415. The numbers refer to the shade of yellow, which matches well to most gold threads.

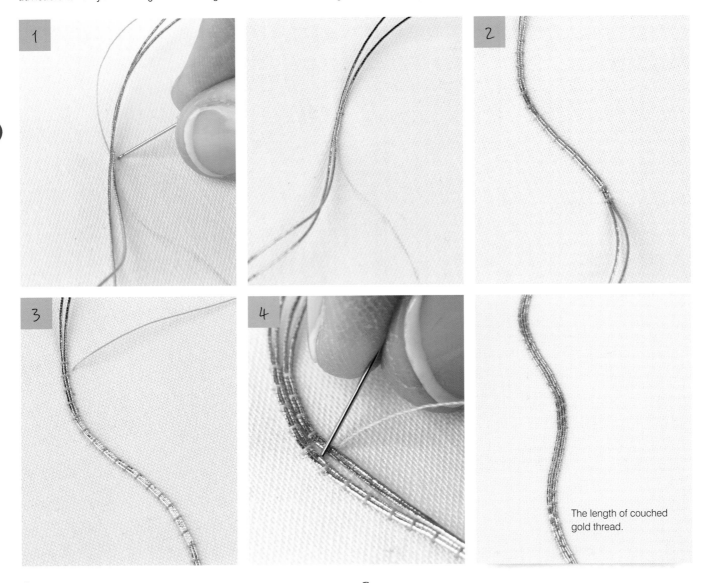

The length of couched gold thread.

1 Lay your threads along the line, placed side by side with the design line through the centre, leaving a tail of about 2–3cm (¾–1¼in) at the end. These ends will later be plunged to the back of the work and secured there.

2 Begin to couch the threads with evenly spaced stitches 2–3mm (¹⁄₁₆–⅛in) apart. Each stitch sits at a 90-degree angle to the threads underneath. These couching stitches should be given a tight tension to hold the threads in position.

3 If an additional row is required, this is placed next to the first row. To work the second row of couching, lay the two new threads next to the first row. Your couching stitches should form a bricked pattern with those of the first row. Bring your needle up a little way from the first row, between the stitches of the previous row.

4 Take your needle down, underneath the gold thread of the first row. Try to angle the needle towards the first row. This will ensure that there are no spaces between the rows. Keep the stitches at a 90-degree angle to the gold threads underneath.

PLUNGING: USING A LASSO

I prefer this method for plunging the ends of the gold thread. It is preferable to use this method for plunging the ends through felt padding or if the ends of the gold thread are very short, and therefore cannot be threaded into a needle. Tails of metal thread should be plunged individually to avoid making holes in the fabric.

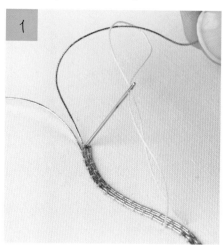
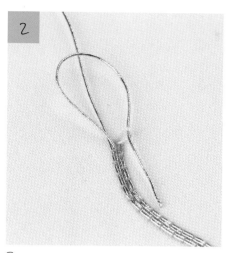
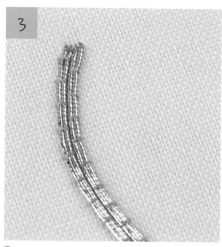

1 Take a length of buttonhole thread and thread the two ends of thread into a chenille needle to form a loop. This loop of thread is called a lasso. Take the needle down at the point where you want the gold to be plunged. Thread only the tip of the gold thread into the lasso.

2 Pull the lasso from the back and gently ease the gold thread to the back of the work. Remove the lasso.

3 This method is repeated to take all the ends to the back. Work methodically along the line, plunging each end individually.

TYING BACK ENDS

Once all of the ends are plunged, they are folded back on themselves and then oversewn in pairs on the back. They are then trimmed away to keep the back tidy and avoid any tangles.

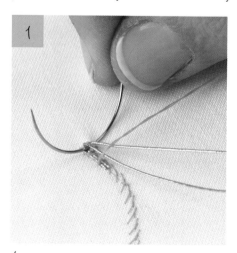
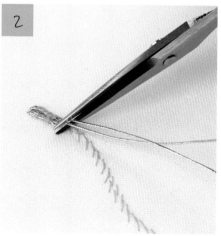

The ends, tied back.

1 Turn your work over to the back. Use a double sewing thread, to give extra strength. Start your thread behind the couched line. Lay the tails of thread back along the couching line. Closely oversew the threads for about 5mm (¼in), catching into the stitching and fabric on the back of the work.

2 Carefully trim away any excess threads on the back.

Note

I usually use a curved needle for tying back the ends; however, some people prefer to use an embroidery needle. Try both and use whichever you prefer.

FLY STITCH

This is a quick and easy stitch to work. Each separate fly stitch looks like a capital 'Y'.

Fly stitch can be worked as single stitches scattered on a design or in a continuous line, worked either close together or more spaced apart. The choice of threads depends on the weight of fabric and effect required. A round twisted thread such as cotton perlé can give excellent results.

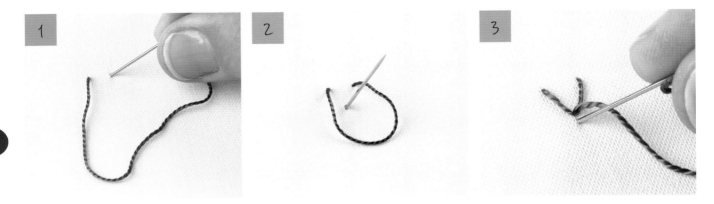

1 Bring your needle out at the top left of where you would like the stitch. Insert your needle back in at the top right, horizontal to where the needle was inserted, making a 'V'-shaped loop.

2 Bring the needle out diagonally between the two stitches.

3 Pull the thread downwards over the working thread.

To secure the loop, work a vertical straight stitch. The length of the tail may be varied to produce different effects.

The completed stitch.

A vertical row of fly stitches.

RIBBON STITCH

Ribbon stitch is a stitch frequently used in ribbon embroidery. The stitches resemble leaves, so are often used to create grasses and foliage.

Experiment with different widths of silk ribbon. Avoid working with lengths of ribbon longer than 20cm (7⅞in) as the ribbon can look worn very quickly. Start with a knot on the back or alternatively start and finish by securing the ribbon on the back with a sewing thread.

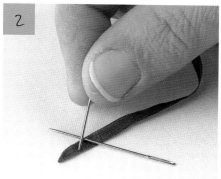

1 Bring your needle up through the fabric at the base of the stitch. Lay your ribbon along the fabric, in the direction of the stitch. Carefully take your needle down through the centre of the ribbon, at the tip of the stitch.

2 Lay a large tapestry needle over the ribbon. This helps to prevent losing the distinctive curl at the end of the stitch.

3 Gently pull the ribbon around the tapestry needle.

Bring your needle up to the top of the fabric ready to work the next stitch. Gently slide the tapestry needle out. The needle is used to prevent you from pulling the ribbon too tightly, losing the curl at the end of the ribbon. However, if the curl is a little large, you can pull the ribbon a little further.

> ## Warning
> If you pull too tightly on the ribbon, you will end up with a straight stitch, which is impossible to correct. If this happens, it is best to unpick the ribbon and start again.

The completed stitch.

Ribbon stitches worked in two ribbons of diffferent colours and widths.

SPIDER'S WEB ROSE

Also known as a woven wheel, a spider's web produces a small woven circle with a raised appearance. It can be stitched with any embroidery thread or silk ribbon.

The wheel is worked in two stages. The first stage is to stitch the 'spokes' of the wheel. Using a matching embroidery thread, start your thread within the circle.

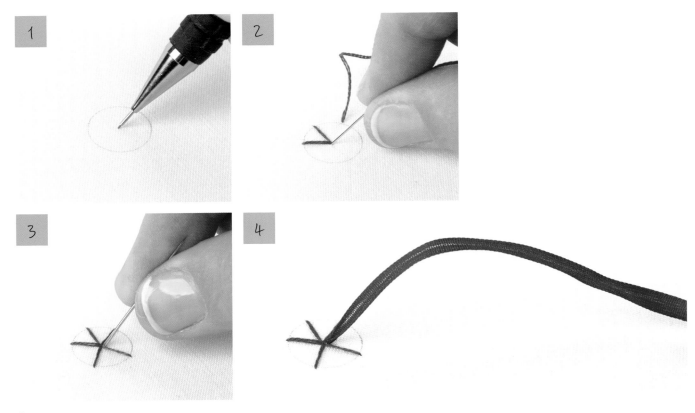

1 Using a pencil or fabric marker, draw a circle on your fabric. It should be a little smaller than the desired size of your woven wheel. Mark the centre of the circle.

2 Stitch an odd number of radiating stitches. I have used two strands of stranded cotton. Use five stitches for a small wheel and seven stitches for a larger wheel. Bring your needle up outside the design line and down into the central point.

3 Continue around until you have stitched all the spokes then finish your thread.

4 Start your silk ribbon following the instructions on page 39. Bring your needle out near the centre of the wheel.

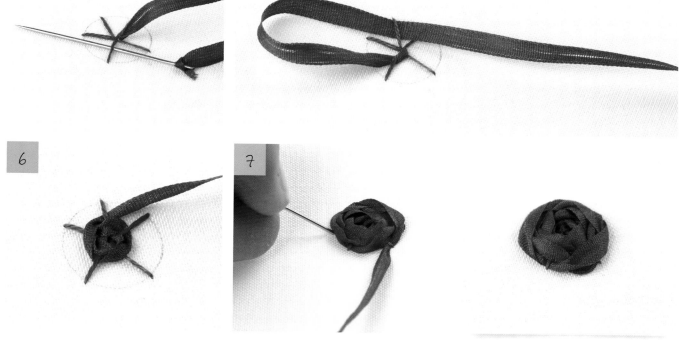

5

6 7

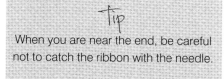

The complete spider's web rose.

5 Weave over the first thread and under the next, and repeat as required. Pull your thread quite tightly to start with, then make later rounds looser so that the ribbon lies flat.

6 Continue weaving around the wheel until all the spokes are covered.

7 When the weaving is complete, insert your needle under the previous round of weaving. Finish the ribbon on the reverse.

> Tip
> When you are near the end, be careful not to catch the ribbon with the needle.

The lid of the *Afternoon Tea Box* (see pages 92–115) features spider's web roses worked in silk ribbon in the top corners, along with ribbon stitch leaves and stem stitch.

55

RAISED LEAF STITCH

This stumpwork stitch is simple to master, and is best worked in a stranded cotton. Experiment with the thickness of card that you use and the number of strands and stitches, to vary the size of each stitch.

Cut a strip of thin card to a width no greater than 1cm (⅜in), and about 4–5cm (1½–2in) long. The card will be used to work the stitches over, but will be removed before the leaf stitch is complete. I have used a strip of card 6mm (¼in) wide.

Draw a single line on your fabric to mark the position of the leaf using a pencil or fabric marker. Take two or more strands of stranded cotton in an embroidery needle and bring your thread out at the tip of the leaf.

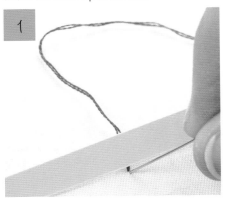

The first stitch over the card. Take care to keep an even tension.

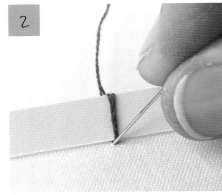

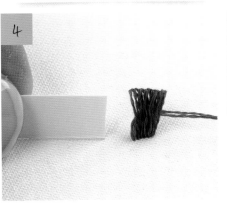

1 Lay your strip of card over the pencil line on its edge. Make the first stitch over the card, taking your needle down in the same hole to where it emerged. This will ensure a sharp point to the leaf.

2 Bring the needle out next to the previous stitch. Take your thread over the card once again and down in the same hole again.

3 Continue stitching over the card along the line, working towards the stem. There should be about four to six stitches in total. The more stitches you work, the larger the leaf will be. Bring your thread out next to the previous stitch. Slide your needle between the stitches and the card back towards the tip of the leaf. Gently pull the thread through.

4 Holding the stitches, carefully remove the strip of card.

The complete stitch.

5 Hold the stitches upright and gently pull the thread over towards the base of the leaf. Take the thread down through the fabric to secure the stitches in place.

CONSTRUCTION STITCHES

Construction stitches are those that are used when physically constructing a box. They are usually worked in a strong, matching thread in a curved needle.

Keep practising these two particular construction stitches using a curved needle – they are often a struggle at first, but persevere and over time they will become easier.

LADDER STITCH

Ladder stitch – also known as slip stitch – is a method of joining two pieces of fabric so that the stitch thread is invisible. Use a sewing thread that is a shade darker than the fabric, to avoid the thread showing.

The stitches should be kept small and the thread pulled tight. Use a curved needle throughout, as it is very difficult to use a straight needle for ladder stitch. For any seams that are likely to encounter excess wear and tear, it is advisable to ladder stitch these twice for extra strength.

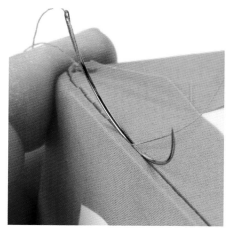

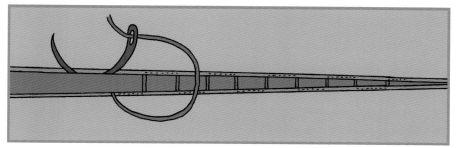

Keep your ladder stitches small and use a fine, curved needle.

HERRINGBONE STITCH

Use herringbone stitch to apply your embroidery fabric to a base fabric (working around the edges), or to attach a fabric hinge securely to your box (see pages 84–85). Herringbone stitch is worked in straight rows from left to right, to create a series of crossed zigzag stitches.

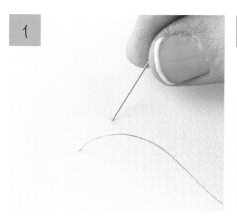

1 Bring your needle up through the fabric on the lower guideline, then make a short stitch from right to left a little further along the top line.

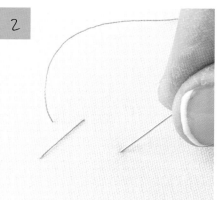

2 Make a second short stitch along the lower line, spacing the stitches evenly. Repeat along the row.

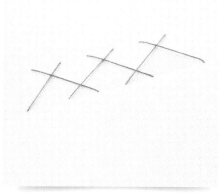

The completed herringbone stitch.

PROJECTS

The three projects in this chapter show you the extensive potential of box construction. I have explored several construction techniques within these three projects, beginning with an explanation of how to construct a basic box, before building up towards more challenging box construction techniques. To obtain the best results, please read all the instructions carefully and refer back to the basic box project if you need to.

All of the box measurements are given for each project, as are templates for the embroidered panels.

You do not have to replicate any of these projects exactly – there are many techniques for you to explore. Why not create your own embroidered box combining several of the techniques? I hope that these projects inspire you to develop your own ideas – the construction techniques can be mixed and matched to suit your design.

Projects to try: below, the *Dragonfly Treasure Chest*; top right, the *Afternoon Tea Box*, bottom right, the *Stumpwork Casket*.

CONSTRUCTING A BASIC BOX

To begin to understand box construction and become familiar with the processes involved, I suggest that you start by working through the steps for this basic box. Every stage is fully explained and this will be your reference as you work through the rest of the projects.

For your first box I recommend making a simple box without the addition of embroidery. Once you understand the principles of box construction, you can include embroidery on the sides and the lid. This basic box measures 7 x 7 x 7cm (2¾ x 2¾ x 2¾in) – I suggest that you follow these dimensions for your first box as this is a manageable size to begin with. A plain cotton fabric or one with a small print works well for this size of box – I have used a Tana Lawn.

The basic execution for all the projects in this book is identical. Other relative information will be explained as necessary for each project. Read everything carefully before you begin each project and revisit this chapter whenever you need to.

YOU WILL NEED:

Two fat quarters of quilting cotton fabric – 50 x 55cm (19¾ x 21⅝in)

30 x 40cm (11¾ x 15¾in) acid-free mountboard

Sewing machine thread to match your fabrics

White craft felt

12mm (½in) wide double-sided tape

Buttonhole thread

Very sharp HB pencil or mechanical pencil

Craft knife with a retractable blade

Cutting mat

Acid-free tissue paper

30cm (12in) metal safety ruler

Curved needle

Ruler

Set square

Small, sharp embroidery scissors

Fabric shears

Paper scissors (for cutting tape)

Glass-headed pins

Gathering the materials

Before you begin your project, it is important to gather everything together – fabrics, threads, construction materials and needles – so that you have everything close to hand.

Do check you have enough fabric to complete the box, allowing extra fabric to wrap around the card pieces.

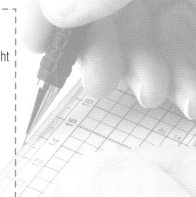

DIMENSIONS

The basis of any handmade box is accurately cut card with 90-degree corners and straight edges. It is important to measure and cut the card to size, following the measurements carefully to ensure that the box fits together.

EXTERIOR	INTERIOR
Lid: 7 x 7cm (2¾ x 2¾in)	**Lid:** 6.2 x 6.2cm (2⁷⁄₁₆ x 2⁷⁄₁₆in)
Front: 7 x 6.8cm (2¾ x 2¾in)	**Front:** 6.6 x 6.6cm (2⅝ x 2⅝in)
Back: 7 x 6.8cm (2¾ x 2¾in)	**Back:** 6.6 x 6.6cm (2⅝ x 2⅝in)
Sides: 6.6 x 6.8cm (2⅝ x 2¾in)	**Sides:** 6.2 x 6.6cm (2⁷⁄₁₆ x 2⅝in)
Base: 6.6 x 6.6cm (2⅝ x 2⅝in)	**Base:** 6.2 x 6.2cm (2⁷⁄₁₆ x 2⁷⁄₁₆in)

DRAWING AND CUTTING THE CARD

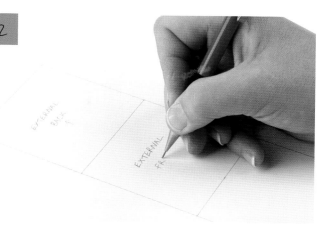

Achieving clean-cut edges

Keep the retractable knife with the blade at a 90-degree angle to the card to use as much of the cutting edge as possible, not just the point. If any rough edges remain, they can be sanded down with fine sandpaper.

1 Draw out the box pieces accurately on mountboard, using a ruler and a set square. If the corners or edges of the mountboard have been damaged, cut a new straight edge and calculate the measurements from the clean, crisp edge to improve accuracy.

2 Label each piece in the centre, indicating the top edge with a directional arrow – this is important.

3 Place the mountboard on a cutting mat and a safety ruler on the pencil line. Apply pressure to the ridged safety ruler to keep it from moving. Use a sharp knife to score the mountboard using the safety ruler to guide you in a straight line. Keep scoring the card until you cut all the way through.

4 Repeat for all the box pieces.

Hints and tips

Measure your card twice and cut once!

Always use a knife with a sharp blade. Change the blade frequently or as soon as it appears blunt.

PADDING

The interior has additional felt padding. The size of the padding is 8mm (⁵⁄₁₆in) less than the size of the box exterior.

DIMENSIONS

Lid: 6.2 x 6.2cm (2⁷⁄₁₆ x 2⁷⁄₁₆in)

Front: 6.2 x 6.2cm (2⁷⁄₁₆ x 2⁷⁄₁₆in)

Back: 6.2 x 6.2cm (2⁷⁄₁₆ x 2⁷⁄₁₆in)

Sides x 2: each 6.2 x 6.2cm (2⁷⁄₁₆ x 2⁷⁄₁₆in)

Base: 6.2 x 6.2cm (2⁷⁄₁₆ x 2⁷⁄₁₆in)

1 Draw out and cut the internal felt pieces, following the measurements above. Write on the reverse of each piece in pencil where the piece is intended to be used.

2 Cut out the pieces using fabric shears.

3 Place a few strips of double-sided tape on each of the internal card pieces, taking care not to cover the label!

4 Carefully position the felt padding and stick in place.

5 Trim away any excess around the card template using the fabric shears.

NOTES ON PADDING THE PIECES

The lid and base pieces are fully padded so the felt is taken to the edges. The side pieces will sit within the front and back pieces, so there is no padding where these two pieces meet.

There is also no felt padding 2mm (¹⁄₁₆in) from the top of the interior box pieces – this allows for the interior lid to sit flush on top of the box.

The padded box pieces.

BASIC BOX PADDING TEMPLATES

The templates show the position of the padding on the internal card pieces. The dotted area indicates the felt padded areas.

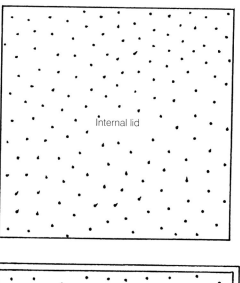

Internal lid

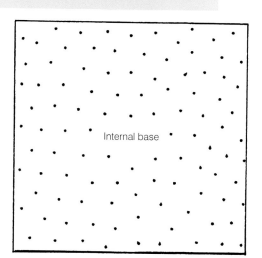

Internal base

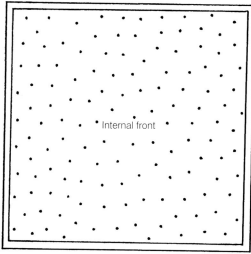

Internal front

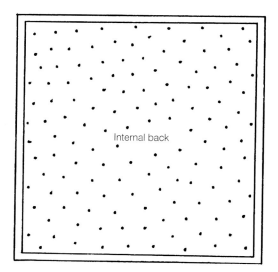

Internal back

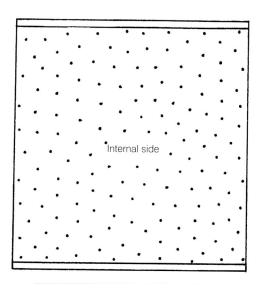

Internal side

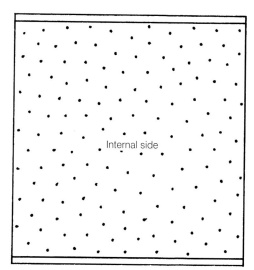

Internal side

COVERING CARD USING DOUBLE-SIDED TAPE

I often cover internal box pieces with plain fabric using double-sided tape, and cover patterned or embroidered fabric for external box pieces by lacing the card on the reverse (see pages 66–67).

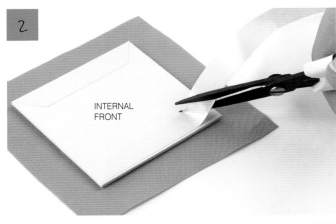

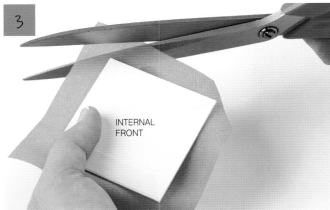

1 Cut a piece of fabric, following the grain. It should be about 1.5cm (⁹⁄₁₆in) bigger than the card on each side.

2 Cut a length of double-sided tape at 45 degrees, then place a piece along both of the long edges, about 1mm (¹⁄₁₆in) in from the edge of the card. The points of the tape should be positioned into the corners of the card.

3 Place the card and fabric face-down on the table with the card straight with the grain of the fabric. To reduce the bulk of fabric on the reverse, cut away the corners of fabric, taking care to cut away only 5mm (¼in) from the corners of card.

4 Remove the paper backing of the double-sided tape. Fold over the excess fabric and stick it down to the double-sided tape on the back. There should be no creases in the fabric.

5 Repeat for the opposite side, pulling the fabric as tight as possible around the card.

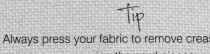

Tip
Always press your fabric to remove creases before covering the card pieces.

6

INTERNAL
FRONT

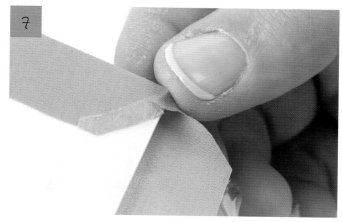

7

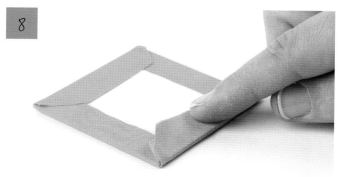

8

9

INTERNAL
BASE

INTERNAL
BACK

INTERNAL
SIDE

INTERNAL
SIDE

INTERNAL
FRONT

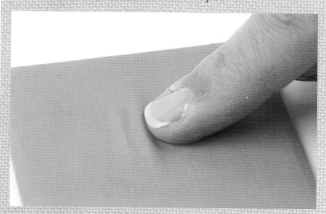

Tip

Ensure that the fabric is pulled taut around the card;
otherwise wrinkles and bubbles will show. To test that the
fabric is taut, run your fingernail along the front of each
piece to check that it is as tight as possible. Readjust the
fabric if necessary.

6 Place two pieces of double-sided tape on the remaining two sides.
The tape will overlap the fabric at the corners. Cut the tape at 45
degrees to the corners.

7 Remove the backing paper from the double-sided tape. To help
achieve a neat corner with no frayed edges the corners will need to be
folded in first. Using your fingernail, fold in the corner of fabric first
and stick in position.

8 Fold over the remaining two sides and stick in place to the double-
sided tape.

9 Repeat for all the other card pieces.

65

COVERING CARD USING THE LACING METHOD

If the fabric you are using is patterned or embroidered, the card pieces need to be covered in a slightly different way to ensure that your pattern or embroidery is placed on the card in the desired position, the grain is straight and there are no wrinkles in the fabric. The reverse is also neat around the outer edge, so this method is ideal for the lid where the edge of the reverse is visible.

When covering card with embroidered or patterned fabric, think carefully about where you place the card before you lace it, so that the pattern is central – the position of the pattern or embroidery is important, and the lacing method ensures this. This method is more time-consuming than taping, and can cause an excess bulk of fabric on the reverse, resulting in the box not fitting together.

If additional padding is required, this needs to be positioned now. This is placed between the card and the embroidered fabric and will help to smooth out any lumps on the back of the embroidery. Cut the padding the same size as the card and hold it in place with a few strips of double-sided tape.

Allow a 2cm (¾in) seam allowance for the exterior lid.

Above: patterned fabric before and after it has been used to cover card.

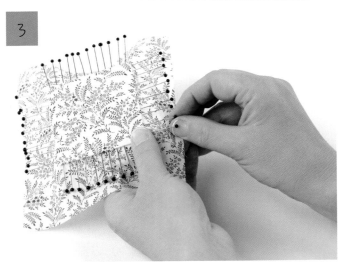

1 Measure your fabric to find the centre of each side and mark with pins. Measure each side of your card and mark with a sharp pencil. Place the fabric over the card and match up the pins with the pencil marks on the edges of the card. Stick the pins from the fabric into the card on all four sides.

2 Stick more pins at 1–1.5cm (⅜–⁹⁄₁₆in) intervals, through the fabric and into the edge of the card, pulling the fabric tight each time to ensure that there are no wrinkles. By working this way, the fabric is kept taut and the grain is kept straight with the edge of the card.

3 Continue pushing pins into the edge of the card until all four sides have no more room. Ensure that you are fully happy with the position of the embroidery or the pattern over the card – if not, readjust as necessary now before you begin lacing.

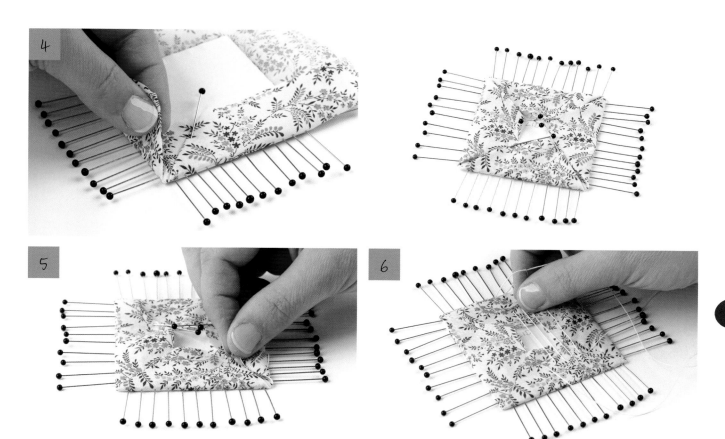

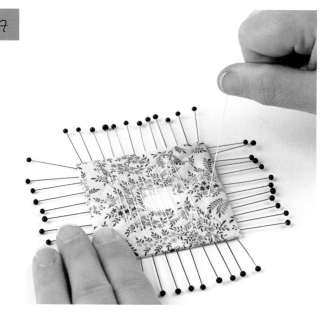

4 Turn over the card so that the fabric is face-down on a sheet of tissue paper. Trim away any excess fabric to 2.5cm (1in) on each side. The corners of the fabric then need folding in so that the fabric is mitred at the corners. Fold in each corner and pin in place but avoid over-stretching the fabric.

5 Fold over the fabric to the back. Using a matching sewing thread in a curved needle, ladder stitch the mitres. Start your thread at the top of the fold and ladder stitch towards the corner. Your stitches should be about 3mm (⅛in) long. Due to the thickness of the card it is not possible to achieve a perfect mitre but it is adequate and will help to keep the fabric flat on the reverse.

6 A strong thread is required to lace the fabric on the back – a buttonhole thread is ideal. Thread your curved needle onto the buttonhole thread on the reel. Do not cut the thread at this stage – the lacing process requires a long length of thread. Starting in one corner, begin lacing the thread from side to side. Do not take your stitches any closer than 5mm (¼in) from the edge of the card. Continue lacing the fabric across the back, pulling the thread through as you go. Finish the thread with a few securing stitches in the opposite corner.

7 Start tensioning the thread to pull the fabric taut. Cut the thread from the reel and thread it onto your curved needle. When you have achieved a tight tension, finish the thread with a few securing stitches.

Tip
To stop the thread catching on the pins at steps 6–8, fold up a sheet of paper tissue and attach to the edge of the lid.

67

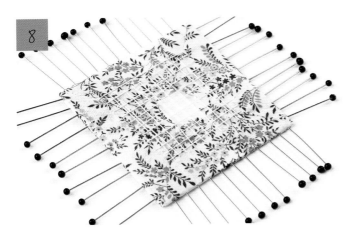

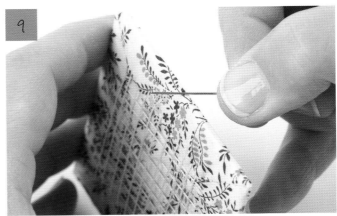

8 Turn your card 90 degrees and repeat the lacing process with the thread on the reel, working across the lacing worked at step 6. Secure the thread in the same way.

9 Remove the pins from around the edge of the card. If any pinpricks remain in the edge of the fabric, they can be scratched away with your fingernail or with the side of a pin.

CONSTRUCTING THE INTERNAL BOX

To obtain a really good fit for your box, it is necessary to work from the inside to the outside so the internal box is constructed first and the external box is built around it.

Use a thread that is darker than the colour of your fabric so that it shows up less, and use ladder stitch (see page 57) to attach each side to the next.

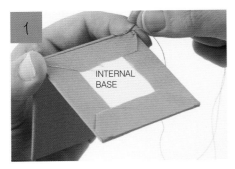

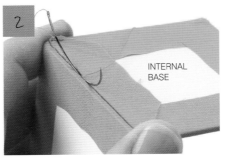

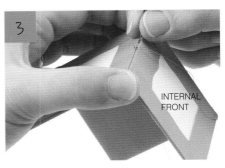

1 Position the side piece against the base piece with the right sides of the fabric facing inwards. I find it easiest to start with these two pieces as the side piece is the same width at the base. Hold both pieces in place with your finger and thumb to ensure that the sides are absolutely level. Start your thread in one corner of the base piece with a knot and a couple of securing stitches.

2 Keeping your stitches about 2–3mm (1⁄16–1⁄8in) long, ladder stitch along the edge of the two pieces. Keep a tight tension on your stitches, so that they do not show.

3 The front piece can now be stitched in place. Continue the ladder stitch with the same thread up the side to the top of the box. Hold the front and side pieces between your finger and thumb and ladder stitch in position. Finish the thread.

4

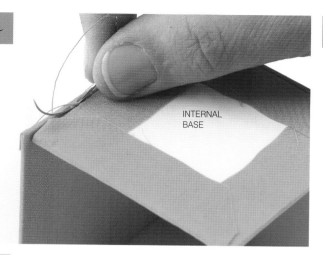

INTERNAL
BASE

5

INTERNAL
SIDE

6

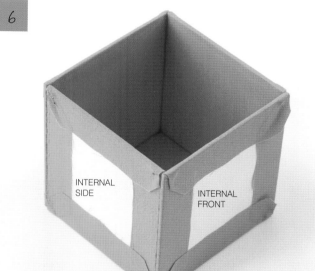

INTERNAL
SIDE

INTERNAL
FRONT

4 The front piece will be 2mm (1/16in) longer than the base piece, to allow for the other side piece to sit within the front. Start a new sewing thread in the corner of the base piece. Ladder stitch the front to the base piece.

5 Start a new thread. Position the second side piece and working from the top of the box downwards, ladder stitch the side piece to the front. Continue stitching the side piece to the base. Finish the thread.

6 Finally, attach the back piece. Start a new thread and position the back piece on top of the sides and base, stitch around the three remaining sides. The internal box is now complete.

STITCHING THE EXTERNAL BOX IN PLACE

Once the internal box is stitched together, the external box can be built around it. Use a single matching thread in a curved needle.

Start the construction of the external box in the same way as for the internal box, making sure that the box pieces are positioned correctly and are the right way up.

1 Thread your curved needle with a matching sewing thread. Ladder stitch the base to the side piece. Your stitches should be about 2–3mm (1/16–1/8in) long. Pull your stitches tight to ensure that they do not show. Take more care with these stitches as they will be visible. Start a new thread. Ladder stitch the side piece to the front up to the top of the box, then finish your thread.

2 Start a new thread in the corner of the front piece and ladder stitch the front to the base piece. The front piece will be 2mm (1/16in) wider than the base piece.

3 Place the internal box inside the three external box pieces, matching up the corresponding sides. Start a sewing thread in the top corner of the front piece.

4 Continue the ladder stitch along the base.

FASTENINGS: MAKING COVERED BUTTONS

Making your own fastenings can add a personal touch to your embroidered box. Use a matching fabric on the buttons to finish off your box perfectly. For added detail, experiment with embroidering the fabric first before covering the button.

Buttons are easily available from most haberdashery departments, in a variety of sizes.

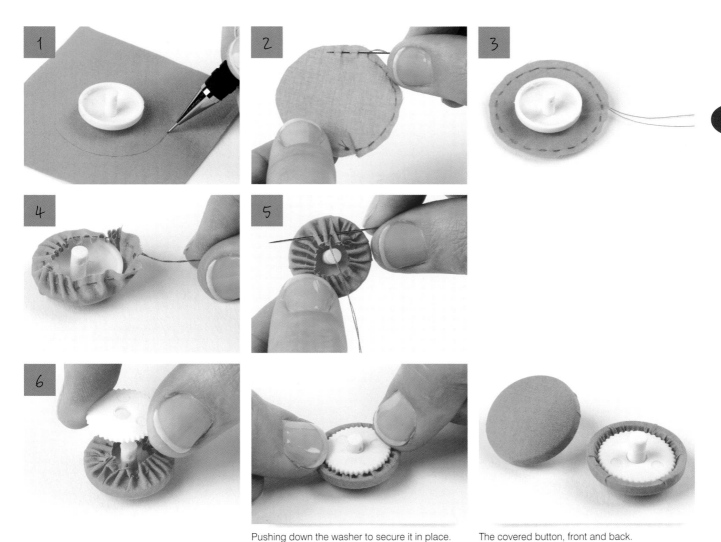

Pushing down the washer to secure it in place.   The covered button, front and back.

1 Cut a circle of fabric about 1cm (⅜in) bigger than the button on each side.

2 Using a matching double thread in an embroidery needle, run a gathering stitch close to the edge of the fabric circle.

3 Place the button in the centre of the gathering stitches on the wrong side of the fabric.

4 Pull the gathering thread firmly around the button. Check that the button is still centred within the fabric circle.

5 Secure the thread tightly on the back and smooth the gathers around the button.

6 Place the washer on the back of the button, pushing it down firmly, to secure it in place.

Dragonfly Treasure Chest

17 x 16.5 x 10cm (6¾ x 6½ x 3¹⁵⁄₁₆in)

This stunning treasure chest enables you to create a simple box that includes a curved lid, a fabric hinge and a secret compartment hidden underneath a false floor. This box builds on the techniques learned in the basic box project and can be used as a progressive project before you move on to more advanced construction techniques.

This box began with the lid, which was constructed from a snack tube, cut in half. After carefully taking several measurements the overall size of the box was created. The technique of making a curved lid could be extended to make a curved spine for a book box.

The lid is embroidered with a few simple stitches and embellished with crystals and beads. The design is inspired by a brooch made from crystals.

The finished box, back view.

The finished box, front view.

TEMPLATE

This template, for the box lid embroidery, is
reproduced at full size.

PREPARATION

Draw and cut the box pieces following the measurements carefully. Press all the fabrics to ensure that there are no creases.

DIMENSIONS

EXTERNAL LID
Front: 17 x 2cm (6¾ x ¾in)
Back: 17 x 2cm (6¾ x ¾in)
Sides x 2: each 9.6 x 2cm (3¾ x ¾in)
Curved lid: 17 x 16cm (6¾ x 6⁵⁄₁₆in)
Curved lid ends: 9.7cm (3¾in) radius

INTERNAL LID
Front: 16.6 x 1.8cm (6⁹⁄₁₆ x ¾in)
Back: 16.6 x 1.8cm (6⁹⁄₁₆ x ¾in)
Sides x 2: each 9.2 x 1.8cm (3⅝ x ¾in)
Lid: 16.6 x 9.2cm (6⁹⁄₁₆ x 3⅝in)

EXTERNAL BOX PIECES
Front: 17 x 9cm (6¾ x 3⁹⁄₁₆in)
Back: 17 x 9cm (6¾ x 3⁹⁄₁₆in)
Sides x 2: each 9.6 x 9cm (3¾ x 3⁹⁄₁₆in)
Base: 16.6 x 9.6cm (6⁹⁄₁₆ x 3¾in)

INTERNAL BOX PIECES
Front: 16.6 x 8.8cm (6⁹⁄₁₆ x 3⁷⁄₁₆in)
Back: 16.6 x 8.8cm (6⁹⁄₁₆ x 3⁷⁄₁₆in)
Sides x 2: each 9.2 x 8.8cm (3⅝ x 3⁷⁄₁₆in)
Base: 16.2 x 9.2cm (6⅜ x 3⅝in)

FLOOR SUPPORTS
Front: 16.2 x 1.5cm (6⅜ x ⁹⁄₁₆in)
Back: 16.2 x 1.5cm (6⅜ x ⁹⁄₁₆in)
Sides x 2: each 8.8 x 1.5cm (3⁷⁄₁₆ x ⁹⁄₁₆in)
False floor x 2: each 16.2 x 9.2cm (6⅜ x 3⅝in)

EMBROIDERY

1 Transfer the design onto pink dupion using the tracing technique (see page 36) and insert the fabric into a hoop frame. Ensure that the fabric is pulled taut while stitching onto the fabric.

2 Create the dragonfly trail in stem stitch using two strands of green stranded cotton. Decrease the stem stitch to a single strand further along the trail.

3 Complete the trail with a running stitch in a single strand of stranded cotton.

4 Using two strands of stranded cotton, scatter French knots within the dotted lines.

5 Scatter the 3mm crystals within the dotted line. Stitch down the crystals with three evenly spaced stitches using an 'invisible' nylon thread (see page 80).

6 The dragonfly is created using the 4mm crystals, stitched closely together. Each crystal is applied using three evenly spaced stitches with an invisible thread in a size 10 embroidery needle.

7 Add extra dimension to the dragonfly by stitching a stem stitch along the edge of the body and wings, using two strands of pink stranded cotton.

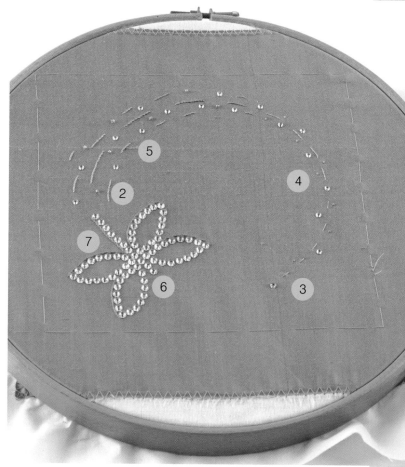

COVERING THE CARD

See pages 64–68 for general instructions on covering card. Cut the fabric on the grain allowing about 1.5cm (⁹⁄₁₆in) for turnings around each side.

The external box pieces are covered in pink silk dupion and the internal pieces are covered in green silk dupion.

1 Cover the internal box pieces including the floor supports with the green silk dupion.

2 Cover the internal lid pieces with green silk dupion.

3 Cover the external box pieces with the pink silk dupion except the external front and back pieces.

4 Pin and lace the pink silk dupion onto the external front and back pieces.

5 Pin and lace the pink silk dupion onto the external back lid.

STITCHING ON THE CRYSTALS

There is such a huge range of beads and crystals available – they can enhance your embroidered work considerably and give it texture.

The crystals are stitched down with three evenly spaced stitches, using an invisible thread.

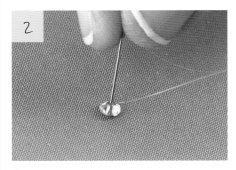 

1 Start your thread securely on the design line and bring up the needle just a little way from the line.

2 Take your needle down through the centre of the crystal pulling the thread firmly. Invisible thread can spring back, so make sure that each stitch sits neatly against the crystal.

3 Bring your needle back up at the edge of the crystal a third of the way round from the previous stitch.

4 Take your needle back down through the centre of the crystal.

5 Secure the crystal to the fabric with one more stitch placed evenly between the two previous stitches.

STITCHING ON BEADS

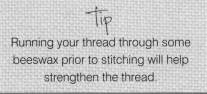

Tip
Running your thread through some beeswax prior to stitching will help strengthen the thread.

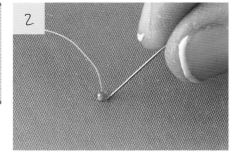 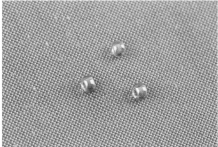

1 Start your thread on the design line or on the reverse. Bring your thread up where you want the bead to sit and thread the bead onto the needle.

2 Push the bead to the bottom of the thread. Take your needle into the fabric at the end of the bead.

3 Secure the thread on the reverse.

BOX CONSTRUCTION

ORDER OF WORK

Generally, this chest is constructed in a similar way to the basic box (see pages 60–73). The internal box is constructed first before the external box pieces are stitched around it.

   This box has a false floor, which rests on floor supports that are stitched in place to all four sides of the internal box pieces.

THE FLOOR SUPPORTS

The floor supports are stitched to the internal pieces before the internal box is constructed. Take care to position each floor support accurately so that the false floor rests smoothly on all four floor supports.

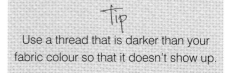

Tip

Use a thread that is darker than your fabric colour so that it doesn't show up.

81

1 Draw a line on the internal side pieces 2mm (1/16in) up from the bottom edge. The floor supports will be stitched to this line.

2 Position the floor support on the line and 2mm (1/16in) in from each side. Using a matching sewing thread in a curved needle, slip stitch the floor supports to the corresponding internal piece around all four sides. The floor supports need to be stitched 2mm (1/16in) up from the bottom edge to allow for the internal base piece.

3 Repeat this process for the other three internal pieces.

CONSTRUCTING THE INTERNAL BOX

1 Position the base piece next to a side piece so that the base sits underneath the floor support. Working from the wrong side, ladder stitch the two pieces together.

2 Place the internal front over the base and side, making sure that the floor supports are level with each other. Continue stitching with the same thread up the side to the top of the box. Finish the thread. Start a new thread in the corner of the base piece and ladder stitch the front to the base, remembering that the front will be 2mm (1/16in) longer than the base piece.

3 Position the second side piece, again aligning the floor support. Working from the top of the box downwards, ladder stitch the side piece to the front. Continue stitching the side piece to the base. Finish your thread.

4 Finally, attach the back piece. Position the back piece against the sides and the base. Start your thread and ladder stitch the three sides of the back piece to the sides and base.

The internal box is now complete.

THE HINGED LID

The lid of this treasure chest sits on top of the sides of the box and is secured to the main box with a fabric hinge. The hinge is made from fabric that matches the material used for the box, and is given extra strength with the addition of a cotton interlining. No interlining is necessary if sturdier fabrics are used.

As the hinge is sandwiched between the external and internal boxes and secured to the external back pieces, the hinge needs to be constructed before the external box is built around the internal box.

The fabric hinge is stitched to the external back and the external back lid pieces.

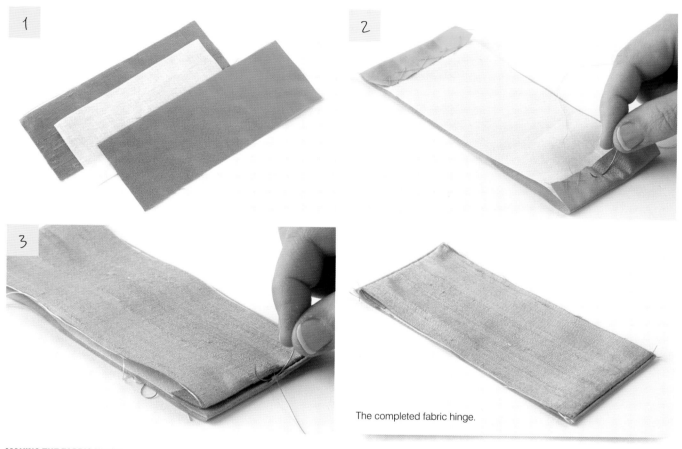

The completed fabric hinge.

MAKING THE FABRIC HINGE

1 Prepare the fabric by cutting two pieces of silk dupion, 19.5 x 7cm (7¾ x 2¾in), one from the external – pink – fabric and one from the internal – green – fabric. Cut a strip of calico or medium-weight cotton fabric 16.4 x 7cm (6⁷⁄₁₆ x 2¾in). This will be used to interline the hinge.

2 Place the interlining onto the external fabric and fold in the two short sides. No turnings are necessary on the two long (internal) sides as these will be secured to the inside of the box. Using a matching single sewing thread in a curved needle, herringbone stitch the turnings to the calico. Take care that the stitching does not come through to the right side.

3 Place the lining fabric onto the wrong side of the hinge, turn in the seam allowances and slip stitch (ladder stitch) the lining in place.

STITCHING THE HINGE IN PLACE

The hinge is stitched to the external back and external back lid pieces. Both of these pieces are covered using the lacing method (see pages 66–68). This is to ensure that you do not stitch through double-sided tape.

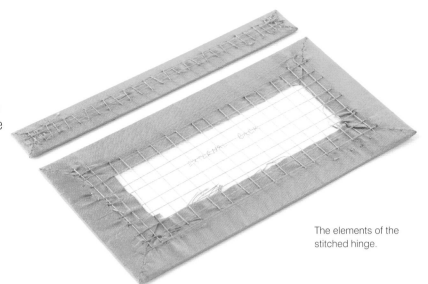

The elements of the stitched hinge.

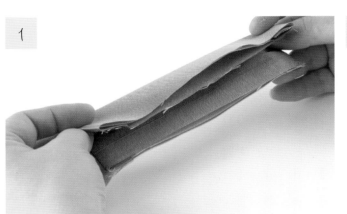

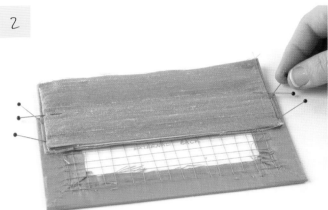

1 Place the external back piece face-down on a piece of tissue paper on your work surface. Gently fold the hinge in half lengthways.

2 Place the hinge face-down onto the wrong side of the external back piece, matching the fold line to the top of the external back piece. Pin the hinge in place.

3 Using a length of buttonhole thread in a curved needle, herringbone stitch the hinge tightly in position, taking the stitching over the ends of the hinge.

4 To avoid excess bulk within the box, trim away the excess fabric from the hinge below the stitching, trimming away the layers at differing places (a, the green dupion, b, the white cotton fabric).

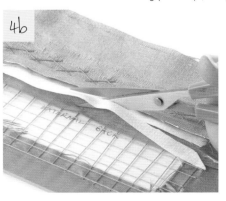

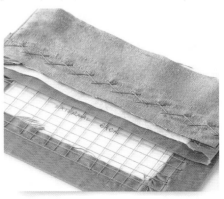

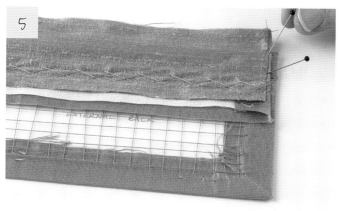

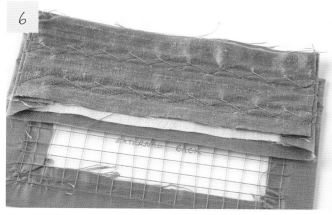

5 Place the external back lid face-down on the table next to the external back piece. Pin the hinge in place.

6 Herringbone the hinge to the external back lid, stitching through all the layers of fabric.

7 Carefully trim off any excess fabric at the top of the hinge.

8 Using a matching thread in a curved needle, stitch the hinge to the edge of the back piece, keeping your stitches small and tight.

9 Repeat the process, stitching the hinge to the back lid piece.

Tip

At step 8, take care that you do not stitch all the way through the hinge – this would result in your stitches showing on the inside of the hinge.

STITCHING ON THE BUTTON JEWEL

The chest is fastened with a ribbon loop and button jewel. The button is secured to the external front by stitching through the fabric and card for added strength. The external front is covered using the lacing technique for added strength and to avoid trying to stitch through the double-sided tape.

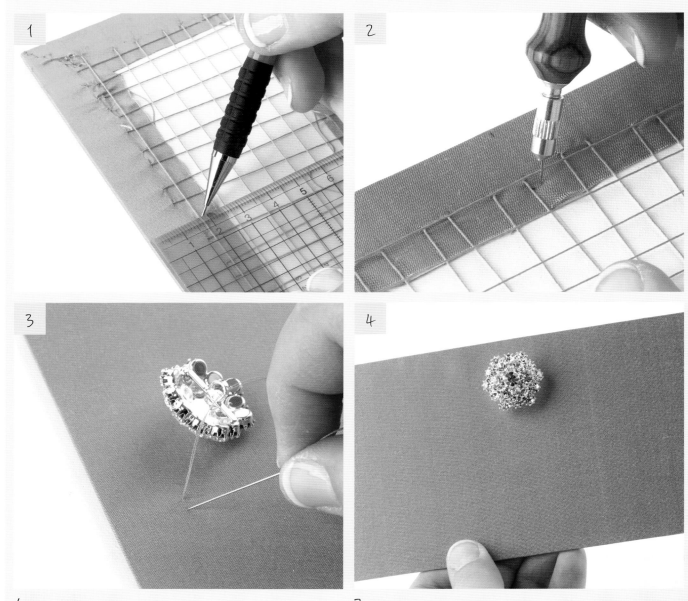

1 Measure the external front card along the width and mark the centre near the top on the reverse with a sharp pencil. The button is stitched 1.8cm (¾in) down from the top edge.

2 To make it easier to stitch through the card, make two holes either side of the button loop through the card using a pricker.

3 Start a double pink sewing thread in an embroidery needle on the back, near the top. Securely stitch the button to the front. You will be stitching through the card and fabric.

4 Stitch several times through the card so the button is very securely attached. Finish the thread on the back.

STITCHING THE EXTERNAL BOX

Once all the external box pieces are prepared, the external box can be constructed around the internal box.

87

Tip

Rest the box on something raised while you stitch, so that you don't squash the button.

1 Hold the base and side pieces between your finger and thumb. Using a matching sewing thread in a curved needle, ladder stitch the two pieces together. Keep your stitches small and tight to ensure that they do not show. Continue the sewing thread and ladder stitch the side piece to the front up to the top of the box. Finish the thread.

2 Start a new thread in the corner of the front piece and ladder stitch the front to the base piece. The front piece will be 2mm (¹⁄₁₆in) longer than the base piece.

3 Place the internal box inside the three external box pieces, matching up the corresponding sides. Start a sewing thread in the top corner of the front piece.

4 Position the second side piece, holding the two pieces between your finger and thumb and ladder stitch from the top edge down towards the base.

5 Continue the ladder stitch along the base.

6 Finally, the back piece is stitched in place. Position the back piece, which includes the hinge and back lid. Ladder stitch the remaining three sides. Finish the thread.

7 To complete the main box and secure the external box to the internal box, ladder stitch around the top edge using a single sewing thread. It is also necessary to stitch the external back to the back of the hinge.

ATTACHING THE RIBBON LOOP

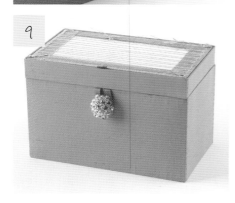

1 Measure the internal front lid piece and mark the centre with a hard, sharp pencil.

2 Cut a length of matching ribbon to 11.5cm (4½in) long. Position the two ends of the ribbon either side of the centre mark, with 7.5cm (2¹⁵⁄₁₆in) of the ribbon showing below the bottom edge of the lid.

3 Attach in place temporarily with a piece of double-sided tape.

4 Position the internal lid on the main box. Check that the loop fits neatly around the button jewel. Readjust if necessary.

5 Secure the ribbon to the internal front with a few securing stitches. Make sure to stitch through the ribbon several times so that it is very securely attached. The external lid can now be constructed around the internal lid.

6 Cover and construct the remaining three external lid pieces around the internal lid. The back lid will be stitched in place later.

7 Stitch the internal lid to the external lid around the rim, using a single pink sewing thread in a curved needle.

8 To ensure that the button loop is securely attached into position, stitch through it several times while stitching the rim.

9 Finally, attach the lid to the main box by stitching the back lid in place.

Note
The size of the ribbon loop depends on the size of your button.
Adjust the loop accordingly.

THE LID

The lid is made in two stages: first, the lower lid is constructed, then the curved lid is secured on top. Construct the internal lid pieces using the lacing method (see pages 66-67).

Position the internal lid centrally on the box.

The embroidery for the lid, from pages 78–79.

COVERING THE CURVED LID

The curved lid is constructed from a snack biscuit tube, which has been cut in half lengthways. Alternatively, you can cut a piece of thin card to size and bend it into shape.

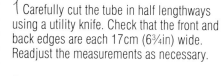

1 Carefully cut the tube in half lengthways using a utility knife. Check that the front and back edges are each 17cm (6¾in) wide. Readjust the measurements as necessary.

2 Apply the pink silk dupion to the pre-shrunk calico.

3 Tack the fabric, cut to the size of the lid, onto the silk with a running stitch using a contrasting sewing thread.

4 Position a piece of white felt over the curved lid and stick it in place with a few pieces of double-sided tape.

5 Remove the embroidery from the frame.

6 Place the embroidery over the cardboard tube, matching up the tacking line with the edges of the card. Hold the fabric in place using fold-back clips. Using a buttonhole thread in a curved needle, work lacing stitches across the sides of the curved lid. Pull the thread tight to ensure that the fabric has no wrinkles or puckers. Finish your thread.

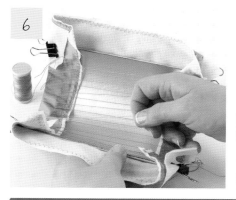

7 Fold in the corners of fabric to the inside of the tube. It is not necessary to mitre the corners. Don't worry if they are a little bulky as they will be hidden inside the lid. Secure the corners to the back of the fabric with a few stitches using a matching thread.

8 Work lacing stitches in the opposite direction to secure the fabric around the curved lid using a buttonhole thread. Before securing the thread, check that the lacing has not pulled the lid too tight by checking that the curved lid fits the lid on the box.

9 Remove the tacked outline carefully, using a pair of tweezers.

Tip

As the curved lid is made from a thinner card than a box, it is not easy to pin into. Using fold-back clips to hold the fabric in place will help while the fabric is being laced around the card. Be sure to protect the embroidery and surrounding fabric from the clips by folding some scraps of fabric underneath the clips.

THE CURVED SIDES

The sides of the curved lid are semi-circles cut from mountboard. To draw an accurate circle, use a pair of compasses and a sharp pencil.

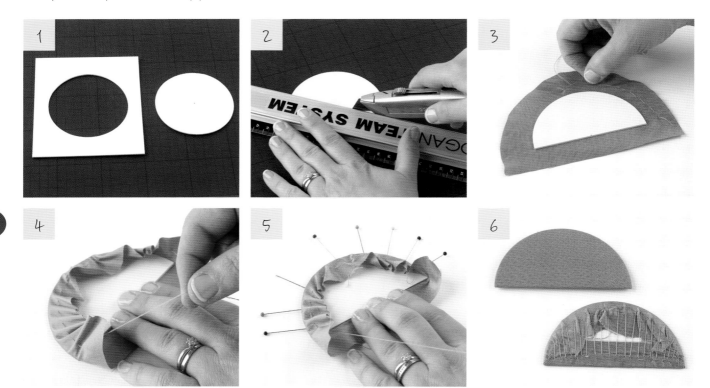

1 Draw a straight line across the centre of a piece of mountboard with a ruler and sharp pencil. Using a pair of compasses and a compass cutter, cut out a circle with a radius of 9.7cm (3¾in), ensuring that the line runs through the middle of the circle. Carefully separate the cut circle from the surrounding mountboard.

2 Align a metal ruler to the centre line and use a utility knife to cut the circle in half to create the two ends of the lid.

3 Cut two pieces of silk, one for each semi-circle of mountboard, including a 1.5cm (⁹⁄₁₆in) seam allowance all around. Ensure that the fabric is cut on the grain. Place down the first piece of mountboard on the semi-circle of silk.

4 Using a double sewing thread, work a running stitch around the curve of the silk about 1cm (⅜in) outside of the card. Start your thread with a large knot. Gently pull the running stitch, which will cause the fabric to gather around the card. Finish the thread.

5 Pin the fabric around the edge of the mountboard semi-circle. Using a length of buttonhole thread, work lacing stitches back and forth across the back to ensure that the silk is pulled tight around the mountboard.

6 Repeat steps 6–8 for the other semi-circle.

FINISHING THE LID

1 Place a semi-circle underneath the curved lid. Secure in position using a matching thread in a curved needle, keeping the stitches small and tight. The semi-circle should sit just below the curved lid. Repeat for the other side.

2 Position the lid on your box and ladder stitch in place.

FITTING THE FALSE FLOOR

The false floor sits on the floor supports. There are two small matching ribbon tabs inserted between the two pieces of card to lift the false floor from the box.

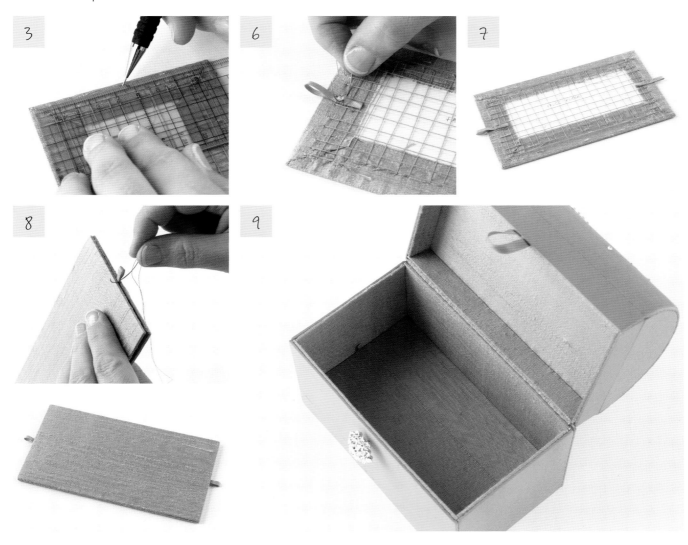

1 Check that the two false floor card pieces fit snugly inside the box. Re-cut if necessary.

2 Cover the card pieces using the lacing method (see pages 66–68) with the green silk dupion. Check again that the pieces sit snugly into the box.

3 Mark the centre along the width on the reverse side of one of the card pieces with a sharp pencil.

4 Cut two pieces of ribbon each 6cm (2⅜in) long. Fold each ribbon in half.

5 Position one ribbon tab over the centre mark with about 1cm (⅜in) showing. Pin in position.

6 Secure the ribbon tab in place with a few stitches. Use a single matching thread in a curved needle and stitch several times through the ribbon. It needs to be very securely attached.

7 Repeat for the ribbon tab on the opposite side, ensuring that both ribbon tabs are the same size.

8 Matching up the sides, place the two pieces of card wrong sides together. Ladder stitch around all the edges using a matching sewing thread in a curved needle. Be sure to stitch through the ribbon each time.

9 Fit the false floor into your treasure chest.

Your treasure chest is now complete!

Afternoon Tea Box

20 x 17.5 x 16cm (7⅞ x 6⅞ x 6⁵⁄₁₆in)

This box was inspired by my visit to Claridge's in London for afternoon tea with my husband. We enjoyed a delicious tea of sandwiches, scones and cakes, but weren't able to finish it all, so we took the remaining cakes home in a beautiful box. I was inspired to make my own tea box, and the colours that I chose to use on this box were inspired by the china that we used. I just loved the green and white with a touch of gold! The inspiration for the embroidered lid is 'Tea in an English Country Garden' featuring rambling roses and a tea set identical to the one that we used at Claridge's.

This hexagonal box comprises eighteen separate external panels and includes an embroidered lid with a raised lining. Inside the box is a tray with gold cord handles sitting on tray supports. The lid is embroidered with applied layered fabrics and decorated with surface stitches and silk ribbon roses.

This box is a real test of your accuracy. For the best results, measure and cut the card as you construct the box. The technique of joining panels together to create one side of the box – shown on pages 109–111 – can be used on any project. For the greatest effect, use contrasting colours.

Opposite:
The finished box with the embroidered lid in place.

YOU WILL NEED:

FOR THE BOX CONSTRUCTION:
Mountboard
Oakshott quilting fabrics – Camargue (cream) and Green Shoot
Matching sewing threads – green and cream
Curved needle
Double-sided tape
Utility knife
Mount cutter
Cutting mat
Pencil
Ruler
Pair of compasses
Fabric scissors
Embroidery scissors
Paper scissors
White felt

Buttonhole thread
Gold cord
Glass-headed pins
Acid-free tissue paper

FOR THE EMBROIDERY:
White cotton backing fabric
Pre-shrunk white cotton fabric
Apple green silk organza
Kiwi green silk organza
Cream linen
White cotton fabric for the tablecloth
Fusible web (e.g. Heat'n'Bond/ Bondaweb)
Blue watercolour paint
Paintbrush
Scraps of cotton fabric – red, beige, brown and pink

Stranded cottons (cream, ecru, white, green, pink, brown, salmon, red, biscuit, grey)
4mm (³⁄₁₆in) silk ribbon – pink
4mm (³⁄₁₆in) silk ribbon – green
Gold passing thread
Gutermann 488 thread
Sewing thread to match the fabrics
Beeswax
PVA (school) glue
Needles – embroidery size 10, chenille size 24, tapestry size 24
Slate frame or hoop frame
Iron and ironing board
Tracing paper
Circle template

TEMPLATE

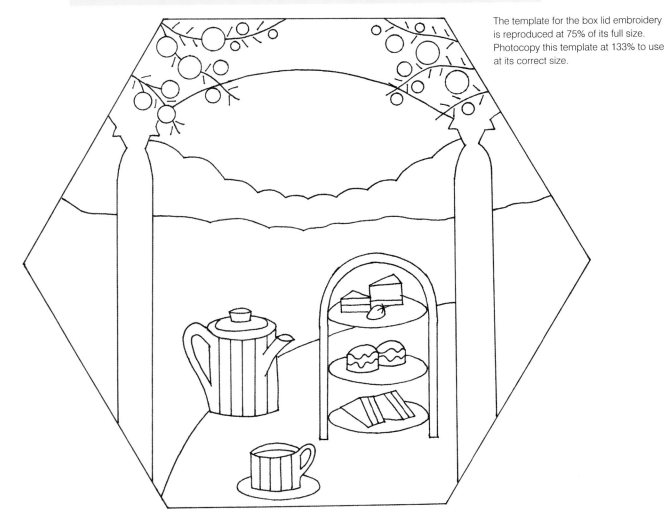

The template for the box lid embroidery is reproduced at 75% of its full size. Photocopy this template at 133% to use at its correct size.

PREPARATION

Draw the design on good-quality tracing paper and mark the centre vertically and horizontally. Use this tracing to help you position the separate elements of the design. Frame up a piece of white cotton background fabric.

1 Iron fusible web onto the back of the scrap cotton fabrics to prevent unwanted fraying.

2 Paint on the fabric using blue watercolour paint – paint only the sky area to avoid the blue paint showing through the green organza.

APPLYING THE ORGANZA LAYERS

1 Place a piece of apple green organza over the design. Using a fine paintbrush, paint a line of glue along the top edge of the design (the foliage). This helps prevent the organza from fraying.

2 Repeat for the kiwi green organza, painting the glue along the lower foliage line.

3 When the glue is dry, carefully cut the organzas through the glued areas, following the design lines.

4 Position the layer of apple green organza on the background fabric and pin it in place, making sure it is smooth.

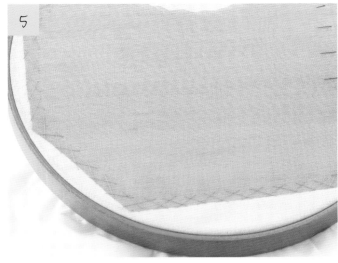

The two layers of organza stitched onto the backing fabric.

5 Secure the organza to the background fabric with some very tiny stitches along the top edge. Use a herringbone stitch to secure the organza in place along the remaining three sides.

6 Position the layer of kiwi green organza using the tracing as a guide if you need to. Pin the organza in place, then secure it to the fabric using the same method as in step 5.

7 Iron some fusible web to the back of a piece of white cotton fabric, for the tablecloth. Using the tracing as a guide, draw a reverse image onto the paper backing. Cut out the tablecloth following the design line – allow about 1cm (⅜in) extra fabric on the right edge, to go underneath the archway, and about 1.5cm (⁹⁄₁₆in) extra fabric along the bottom edge.

8 Peel away the paper backing.

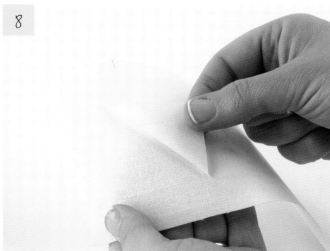

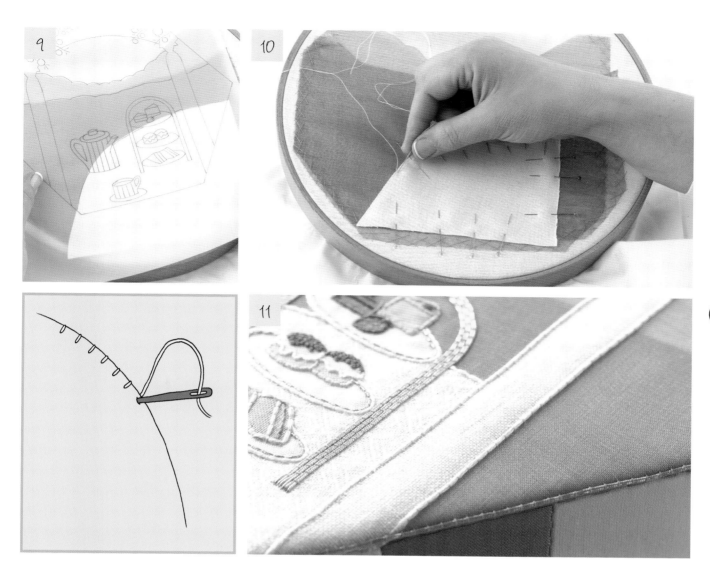

9 Position the tablecloth, again using the tracing as a guide.

10 Pin the tablecloth in place.

11 With a single white sewing thread, secure the tablecloth to the design using small stab stitches (see adjacent diagram). Use a herringbone stitch along the right side, underneath the arch and along the bottom edge. Iron some fusible web onto the back of a piece of linen for the arch. Transfer the design onto the paper backing, using your template as a guide. Cut out the arch carefully using a sharp pair of scissors to get into the corners. Allow extra fabric at the top and bottom edges to turn to the back of the card. Position the arch over the top of the other fabrics using the tracing as a guide, and pin in place. Finally, use a single matching sewing thread to stab stitch the arch in place. The stitches should be about 2–3mm (1/16–1/8in) apart.

EMBROIDERY

Tighten the frame before working the embroidered elements.

1 Mark out a hexagon on the background fabric with a running stitch in a contrasting sewing thread, using the tracing as a guide.

2 Separate all six strands of a long length of cream stranded cotton (see page 38). Using a single strand in an embroidery needle, couch over five strands of stranded cotton around the arch. The threads should cover the raw edges of the archway so don't make your stitches too small. Keep your stitches 3–4mm (⅛–³⁄₁₆in) apart.

3 Prick and pounce the cake stand shape onto the design (see page 37). Draw in the shape with a hard, sharp pencil (such as a 3H or 4H). You need only draw the outer edges of the cake stand.

4 Couch a double length of gold passing thread around the outer edge of the cake stand using a single waxed yellow sewing thread. Working inwards, repeat for the other two rows.

5 Plunge the ends of the passing thread and sew the ends back behind the cake stand.

6 Cut out the three cake plates, teapot and tea cup from cream cotton fabric.

7 Using the tracing as a guide, position the elements and stab stitch in place.

8 Cut strips of green cotton fabric for the stripes on the teapot and cup and stitch in place with a few stab stitches.

9 Cut sandwiches, scones, cakes and strawberry from the scraps of fabric. Position and stitch in place.

10 Couch around all the remaining raw edges, with matching stranded cotton. Use a single strand in the needle over three or four threads. Plunge any ends to the back and secure neatly.

11 Couch a single length of gold passing on the rim of the plates, around the rim of the saucer, around the knob on the lid and the spout of the teapot, using a single yellow waxed sewing thread.

12 Add details to the embroidery as follows:

a) Satin stitch the base on the strawberry mousse cake using a single strand of biscuit stranded cotton.

b) Satin stitch a strawberry on the mousse cake using a single strand of red stranded cotton.

c) Stitch the leaves on the strawberry with three lazy daisy stitches in a single strand of green stranded cotton.

d) Add pips to the strawberry using a single strand of pale green stranded cotton.

e) Add bullion knots on the chocolate cake using one strand of brown stranded cotton.

f) The jam on the scones is created with French knots stitched closely together using two strands of red stranded cotton.

g) Stem stitch a line on each sandwich using a single strand of salmon stranded cotton.

h) To create the tea within the cup, use a single strand of beige stranded cotton, work a long and short stitch horizontally within the tea cup.

i) Add extra dimension to the embroidery by stitching grey horizontal shadow lines beneath the teapot and tea cup, using a single strand of grey stranded cotton.

13 Transfer the design onto your embroidery for the roses using a circle template, keeping the embroidered roses within the hexagon shape. Use a very sharp pencil and carefully draw each circle on the fabric.

14 Stitch spider's web roses (see pages 54–55). Use a single strand of pink stranded cotton to stitch five spokes within each circle. Use a pink 4mm silk ribbon in a tapestry needle for the flowers, weaving under and over the spokes to create the roses.

15 Using two strands of brown stranded cotton, work a stem stitch in two strands for branches.

16 Add leaves to the branches between the roses in ribbon stitch using a green silk ribbon in a chenille needle.

17 Couch a double gold passing thread around the edge of the hexagon using a single waxed yellow sewing thread. Plunge the ends to the back and secure with a few stitches. Trim away any tails of thread.

BOX CONSTRUCTION

Boxes with more than four sides are constructed slightly differently from those with only four. The card is cut using a mount cutter.

CUTTING THE CARD

As the sides of this hexagonal box have corners with angles of more than 90 degrees, every other panel of card has to be cut at an angle, to allow each side to butt onto the next. I have used a mount cutter to cut the pieces of card. The main difference when using a mount cutter is that better results are achieved from cutting the card with one definite, single gliding motion – a smooth, sharp edge will not result from repeated attempts at the same cut. Be sure to change the blade regularly.

DIMENSIONS

INTERIOR PANELS AND TRAY SUPPORT

Cut six each of the following:

Side: 9.7 x 13cm (3¾ x 5⅛in) – cut three per side with straight edges, three per side with bevelled edges

Tray support: 9.4 x 5.6cm (3¾ x 2³⁄₁₆in)

USING A MOUNT CUTTER

1 Place your card on a cutting mat. Measure and mark out your card pieces on the reverse side of the card, using a very sharp pencil.

2 Align the ruler of the mount cutter with one of the marked-out lines on the board. This should be done carefully and accurately before cutting. Apply pressure to the ruler. Push the cutter along the ruler slowly and firmly to cut through the card. You must ensure that you cut through the card at your first attempt, as having a second try will leave a ragged edge.

3 Turn your card around and repeat for the other side.

4 The top and base edges of the internal side pieces are cut out in the usual way using a utility knife.

5 Repeat this process for the other five sides.

Above:

Straight cut card (top) and bevelled cut card (bottom).

THE TRAY SUPPORTS

The tray supports are cut in exactly the same way as the side panels – three pieces of card should have bevelled edges, three should have straight edges.

These are smaller than the internal side pieces as they sit inside the internal box.

CUTTING THE INTERIOR HEXAGON BASE

DIMENSIONS

Radius: 9.5cm (3¾in)

The hexagonal base, cut out.

1 Using a pair of compasses and a very sharp pencil, draw a circle of 9.5cm (3¾in) radius on the card. Mark the radius points around the circumference.

2 Join these points together to make your hexagon.

3 Cut out the hexagon using a utility knife, remembering only to score the card the first time, then press heavily the second time. The blade will remain in the tramline and cut a clean edge.

COVERING THE INTERNAL BASE

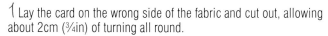

1 Lay the card on the wrong side of the fabric and cut out, allowing about 2cm (¾in) of turning all round.

2 Place long strips of double-sided tape on two opposite sides of the card, cut the tape at 45 degrees and peel off the backing. Fold over the fabric and stick to the tape, pulling the fabric tight and ensuring that the grain of the fabric is straight with the edges of the card.

3 Place two more strips of double-sided tape on two opposite sides of the card. Fold over the fabric again and stick to the tape, ensuring that the fabric is pulled tight.

Repeat this process for the two remaining sides, ensuring that the fabric is pulled tight.

Tip

To reduce some of the bulk, trim away the corners of fabric, taking care not to cut too close to the card.

ATTACHING THE BASE TO THE INTERNAL BOX

The base of the box will then be fitted into the sides. Assembly has to be carried out in this order to ensure that the base is a good fit.

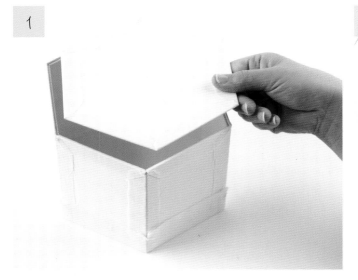

1 Turn the interior box upside-down. Place the interior base into the box so that it sits just within the interior, and rests on the tray supports.

2 Using a matching sewing thread in a curved needle, ladder stitch the base in position.

The internal box is now complete.

EXTERNAL BOX

The external box is made up of nineteen separate pieces, not including the lid. These comprise eighteen individual panels and the base. Each side of the box is made up of three panels of card, covered and stitched together in an alternating colour formation.

For complete accuracy, cut the external side pieces at the same time as the external lid pieces as the sides of the lid sit flush with the sides of the box.

For a simpler box, use the same colour throughout, cutting the external sides as one piece, adjusting the measurements as necessary.

DIMENSIONS

Cut six each of the following:

EXTERNAL SIDE
9.9 x 12cm (3⅞ x 4¾in) – all bevelled (see pages 100–101)

EXTERNAL LID
9.9 x 3cm (3⅞ x 1³⁄₁₆in)

1 Mark the measurements for the external sides and lid panels on mountboard, using a sharp pencil. Cut out the card using the mount cutter on a cutting mat, so that all the edges are bevelled.

2 Once the external side and lid pieces have been cut, each piece needs to be cut into three equal sections. These are then covered in fabric and stitched together to create the external sides of the box.

3 Measure the card and divide each section into three pieces using a sharp pencil. Each section should measure 3.3cm (1⅝in) wide.

4 Place the side piece on a cutting mat and using a metal ruler and a utility knife, cut though the card to create three sections of equal width. Label each piece to indicate the colour of fabric to be used. Repeat for the other side pieces.

5 Place the external lid pieces to one side – you will cover these with fabric later.

6 Cover the external side pieces using double-sided tape (see pages 64–65). Take extra care that the grain of the fabric runs parallel with the sides of the card – cut each piece of fabric in the same direction.

Three panels for one side of the box, sewn together.

Three panels for an adjacent side of the box with alternating panels, sewn together.

7 Ladder stitch the panels together. Start a single sewing thread in a curved needle on the reverse of the panels and slip stitch the panels together on the right side, alternating the colours. Keep the stitching small and tight: each stitch should be about 3–4mm (⅛–³⁄₁₆in) long.

8 Continue the stitching around the edge of the card to achieve a very neat finish.

9 Once all of the panels have been created, the sides can be stitched together, down the side seams. Stitch the panels together in one long strip. Position the external side panels around the internal box and ladder stitch the final seam.

The external side pieces should sit 2mm (¹⁄₁₆in) below the top edge of the base. This is to allow for the external base to sit within the side pieces. For complete accuracy, measure the base and cut the external base accordingly.

ATTACHING THE EXTERNAL BASE AND BOX

Cut and cover the external base in the same way as the internal base (see page 102).

1

DIMENSIONS

Radius: 9.8cm (3⅞in)

1 Turn the box upside-down again and place on a piece of tissue paper. Position the base within the sides of the external box. For a more professional finish, make sure that the straight grain of the internal box is the same as the grain of the external box. Use a matching sewing thread and ladder stitch into position.

2 To complete the main box, ladder stitch the external and internal boxes together. Start a sewing thread in a curved needle just under the top of the external box and ladder stitch the edge of the external box to the raised lining on the internal box.

2

The external box with all side panels stitched in place.

THE LID

The lid is constructed in a similar way to the external sides. However, as the sides of the lid sit flush with the sides of the box, the internal lid must lie well in from the edge of the lid to allow the raised lining to sit comfortably, otherwise the lid will not sit flush. The pieces are covered in the usual way; however, the external lid pieces need extra fabric on the reverse as this will be visible inside the lid.

DIMENSIONS

INTERNAL LID TOP

Radius: 9.5cm (3¾in)

Cut six each of the following:

INTERNAL LID PANELS

9.7 x 1.7cm (3¾ x ¾in)

1 Cover the internal lid sides and top in the usual way using the cream fabric.

2 Ladder stitch the sides together.

3 Insert the internal lid top into the internal lid sides so that the top edges are flush. Secure the internal lid in place with a ladder stitch around the top edge using a matching sewing thread in a curved needle.

4 Take the eighteen external lid pieces and separate them according to colour. Cut out the fabric following the grain, adding 3cm (1³⁄₁₆in) for turnings along the bottom edge and 1.5cm (⁹⁄₁₆in) around the remaining sides.

5 Cover the external lid pieces in the same way as the internal box sides.

6 Stitch the external lid side pieces together, alternating the green and cream panels.

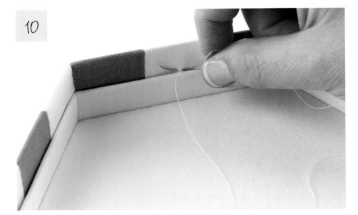

7 Start a single cream sewing thread in a curved needle on the reverse of the panel at the top. Starting at the top, ladder stitch the panels together on the right side keeping the stitches small and tight. Continue the ladder stitch around the bottom edge and up the other side on the reverse of the panel. This is necessary to achieve a neat finish inside the lid of the box. Make sure that the card cut at 45 degrees is placed to the sides of each set of three panels.

8 Repeat the steps to make six sides of the external lid.

9 Join the sides together to form a strip of alternating lid pieces.

10 Position the external lid around the internal lid so that the top edges are flush and ladder stitch the final seam in place.

11 Secure the internal lid to the external lid around the inside rim of the lid. This is a little bit fiddly but necessary to join the internal lid to the external lid.

ATTACHING THE LID

1 Remove the embroidery from the frame.

2 Measure the top of the box and cut the exterior lid from card.

3 Add extra padding to the lid by placing a piece of white felt on the card. Stick in place with a few pieces of double-sided tape.

4 Position the embroidery over the felt padding and place pins through the fabric into the edge of the card. Add more and more pins gradually until a tight tension is achieved. The couched gold passing should be positioned on the edge of the card. Take care when placing pins into the edge so as not to damage the gold thread.

5 Turn over the embroidery and place it on some tissue paper. To help reduce the bulk, carefully trim back the backing cotton fabric only, to the size of the card – take extra care not to cut through any of the other fabric layers.

6 Fold in the corners of the fabrics and, using some buttonhole thread in a curved needle, lace the back (see pages 66–68).

7 Remove the tacking thread from around the edge of the embroidery.

8 Remove the pins. Gently, using your fingernail, stroke the edge of the card to remove the pin pricks. Position the lid on the box. The lid should be positioned with the straight grain of the embroidery the same as the internal and external bases.

9 Secure the lid to the box around all the sides with a small, tight ladder stitch.

DIMENSIONS

EXTERNAL LID TOP
Radius: 10cm (3^{15}⁄$_{16}$in)

6

THE TRAY

The tray inside the box rests on the tray supports. It should be a little smaller than the internal box, to ensure that it can be lifted out smoothly. As the tray is sunk into the box, it is necessary to have a means of lifting the tray out of the box – small gold cord handles are attached to the internal tray and secured in position between the external and internal sides of the tray. Alternatively, tabs can be made from ribbon.

I have used green fabric for the sides of the tray and cream fabric for the bases.

DIMENSIONS

Cut six of each of the following: Cut one of each of the following:

INTERNAL TRAY COMPONENTS

9.1 x 2.8cm (3⁹⁄₁₆ x 1⅛in)

INTERNAL BASE

Radius: 8.9cm (3½in)

EXTERNAL TRAY COMPONENTS

9.4 x 3cm (3¾ x 1³⁄₁₆in)

EXTERNAL BASE

Radius: 9.2cm (3⅝in)

3

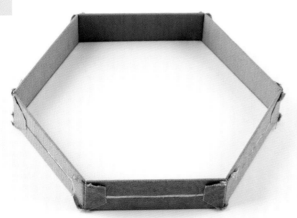

4

5

1 Cover the pieces of card using double-sided tape (see pages 64–65).

2 Construct the internal tray in the same way as the internal lid (see page 112).

3 Cover the internal base and stitch in place. Check the tray fits inside the box; adjust as necessary. There should be ample space around the tray to allow for the external pieces to be stitched in place.

4 Cut two lengths of gold cord each 9cm (3⁹⁄₁₆in) long. Position the gold cord 1.5cm (⁹⁄₁₆in) from the corner of the box. There should be 6cm (2⅜in) of the cord visible from the top of the tray.

5 Stick tape onto the ends of the cord to stop them unravelling, then attach the gold cord securely to the internal tray, using a double sewing thread in a curved needle. The tape should be removed after stitching.

6 Construct the external tray around the internal tray. Now the external base can be stitched in place. For a more professional finish, position the external base so that the grain of the internal base is the same as the grain of the external base.

6

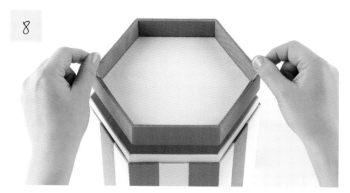

8

7 Complete the tray by stitching around the rim to join the internal components to the external components. To give extra strength to the cord handles, stitch through the cord several times.

8 Insert the tray into your tea box.

Stumpwork Casket

20.5 x 16 x 24cm (8¹⁄₁₆ x 6⁵⁄₁₆ x 9⁷⁄₁₆in)

The ultimate embroidered box has to be an embroidered casket, especially popular during the seventeenth century. Having been inspired to make my own, I spent a morning at the Victoria and Albert Museum in London, studying historial caskets. Some were intricately shaped, others were a simple rectangular box with a lid.

I have based my casket on those typical of the seventeenth century but have added my own twist to it. While trying to emulate the typical colours of the period, I chose to embroider the design with navy, blue, green, cream and gold threads. Each embroidered panel is embellished with gold spangles.

This casket introduces a number of more advanced construction techniques along with a variety of embroidery stitches. A silk dupion or fine cotton lawn would work well for the interior of this box.

There are over 120 card pieces in this box. Work methodically through the project and follow the instructions carefully.

YOU WILL NEED:

FOR THE BOX CONSTRUCTION:
Mountboard
Satin
Red silk dupion
Matching sewing thread
Double-sided tape – 6mm (¼in) wide
Red ribbon to match the silk dupion
Cutting mat
Metal ruler
Utility knife
Mount cutter
Curved needle
Pencil
Fabric scissors
Embroidery scissors
Paper scissors

Glass-headed pins
Stiletto
Mellor
Screwdriver
Pricker
Tweezers
Sandpaper
PVA (school) glue and paintbrush
    for application
Gold drawer knobs with rings x 5
Lock, key and escutcheon
Brass hinges x 4
Feet x 4
Fastening (for top lid)
Mirrored acrylic – cut to 19.7 x 15.5cm
    (7¾ x 6⅛in) – with holes drilled in all
    four corners

FOR THE EMBROIDERY:
White cotton backing fabric
No. 5 gold passing thread
4mm (³⁄₁₆in) silk ribbon – red
Stranded cottons – navy, blue, teal,
    green, cream, red, pink
3mm (⅛in gold spangles
Gutermann 488 thread
Green paper-covered wire (28-gauge)
Wooden beads
Beeswax
Needles – embroidery sizes 9 and 10,
    chenille size 24, tapestry size 24
'Invisible' (nylon) thread
Padding
Acid-free tissue paper
Tracing paper

PREPARATION

1 Press your fabrics to ensure that there are no wrinkles or creases.

2 Frame up some white cotton backing fabric in a slate frame. Apply the satin fabric panel pieces, allowing extra for seam allowances.

3 Transfer your design onto the background fabric using the prick and pounce method (see page 37) or the tracing method (see page 36). Label each embroidered panel on its reverse with a letter, following the legends in the 'Dimensions' lists.

THE EMBROIDERED PANELS

This box has twenty-three embroidered panels. All of the external panels are worked in a similar way (see page 126). The internal panels and the top of the lid have the addition of long and short stitch.

DIMENSIONS OF PANELS

LIDS

a) Top lid: 15.4 x 11.2cm (6$\frac{1}{16}$ x 4$\frac{7}{16}$in) – see template a), page 120

b) Upper lid – front and back: 15.4 x 2.8cm (6$\frac{1}{16}$ x 1$\frac{1}{8}$in) – see template b), page 120

c) Upper lid – sides x 2: each 10.8 x 2.8cm (4$\frac{1}{4}$ x 6$\frac{1}{16}$in) – see template c), page 120

d) Middle lid – front and back: both 15.2 / 20.5 x 4cm (6 / 8$\frac{1}{16}$ x 1$\frac{9}{16}$in) – see template d), page 121

e) Middle lid – sides x 2: each 10.8 / 16 x 4cm (4$\frac{1}{4}$ / 6$\frac{5}{16}$ x 1$\frac{9}{16}$in) – see template e), page 121

f) Lower lid – front and back: 20.5 x 3.5cm (8$\frac{1}{16}$ x 1$\frac{3}{8}$in) – see template f), page 121

g) Lower lid – sides x 2: each 15.9 x 3.5cm (6$\frac{1}{4}$ x 1$\frac{3}{8}$in) – see template g). page 121

DOORS

h) and i) Doors x 2: each 10.2 x 13.5cm (4 x 5$\frac{5}{16}$in) – see templates h) & i), page 122

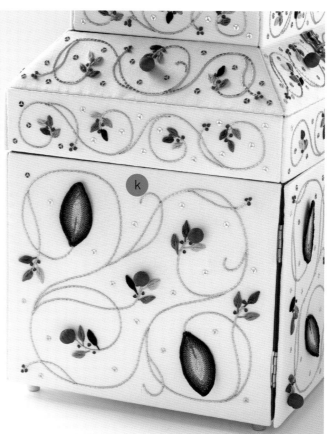

BACK PANEL

j) Main box back: 20.5 x 13.5cm (8¹⁄₁₆ x 5⁵⁄₁₆in) – see template j), page 123

MAIN BOX SIDES

k) Sides x 2: each 15.6 x 13.5cm (6⅛ x 5⁵⁄₁₆in) – see template k), page 124

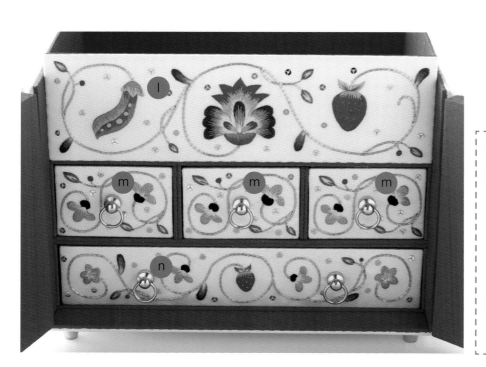

TOP COMPARTMENT AND DRAWERS

l) **Top fascia:** 19.6 x 5.6cm (7¾ x 2³⁄₁₆in) – see template l), page 125

m) **Middle drawers** x 3: each 6 x 4cm (2⅜ x 1⁹⁄₁₆in) – see template m), page 125

n) **Bottom drawer:** 19.1 x 3.5cm (7½ x 1⅜in) – see template n), page 125

TEMPLATES FOR EMBROIDERED PANELS

The design lines for the three-dimensional elements have not been included on the design templates as these will not need to be transferred onto the background fabric.

a) Top lid

b) Upper lid – front and back

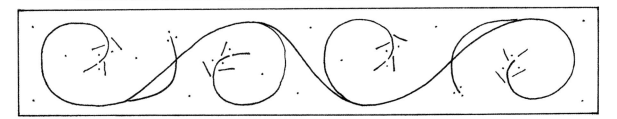

c) Upper lid – sides x 2

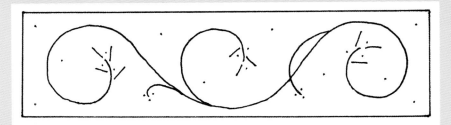

d) Middle lid – front and back

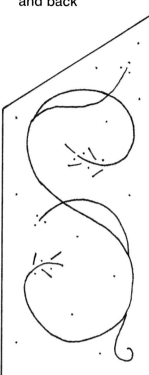

TOP

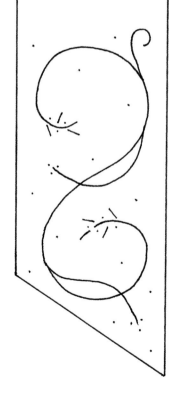

e) Middle lid – sides x 2

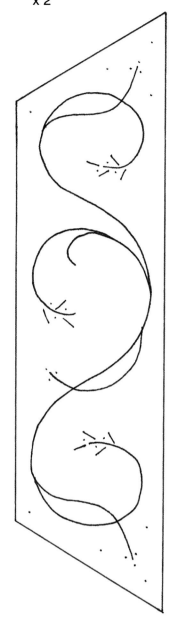

f) Lower lid – front and back

g) Lower lid – sides x 2

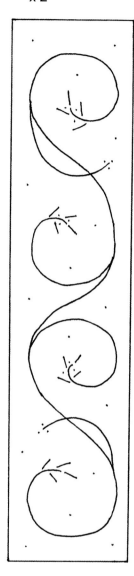

h) and i) Doors

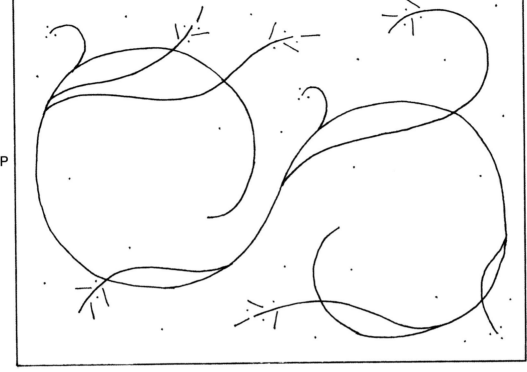

h) Right door

TOP

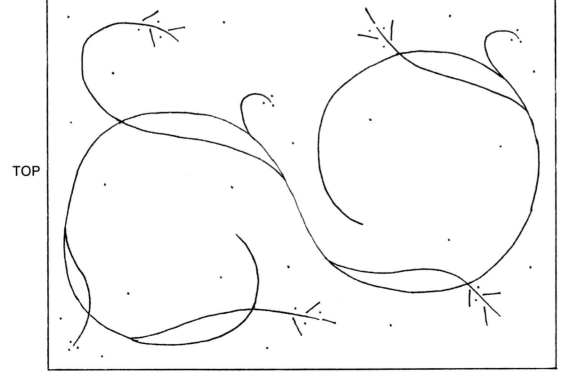

i) Left door

TOP

122

j) Main box back

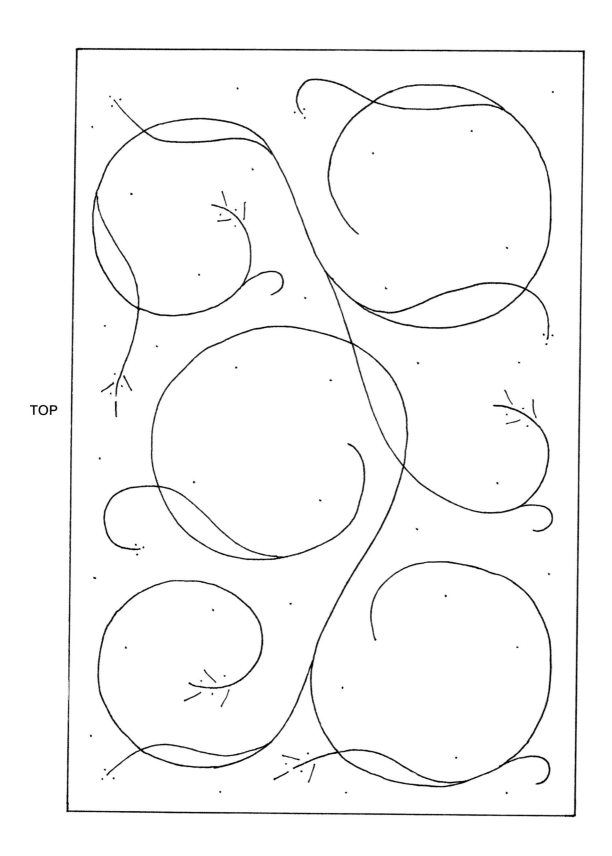

TOP

k) Main box sides

Note

The template below reflects the left side panel of the casket. Tracec
and use a mirror-image copy of this template for the right panel.

TOP

l) Top fascia (above drawers)

TOP

m) Middle drawers x 3

n) Bottom drawer

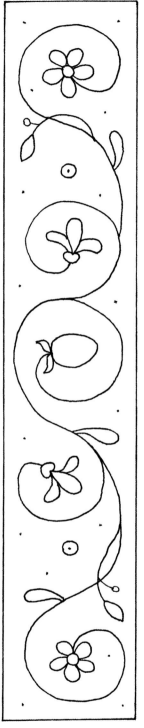

TOP

125

EMBROIDERY

1 Couch a double length of gold passing thread along the swirls, using a single waxed yellow sewing thread in a size 10 embroidery needle.

2 Plunge the ends of gold thread through to the back using a loop of buttonhole thread in a chenille needle. Secure all the tails of thread by oversewing them to the back of the work, using a double length of yellow sewing thread. Trim away any excess thread.

3 Work long and short stitch within the flowers, fruits and insect motifs (see right).

4 Create raised leaf stitches around the ends of the swirls in either two or thread strands of stranded cotton in a size 9 embroidery needle. Use a variety of colours.

5 Scatter French knots between the leaves using 4mm silk ribbon in a size 24 chenille needle.

6 Apply gold spangles to your design (see page 127) using three straight stitches in a yellow sewing thread in a size 10 embroidery needle.

7 Wrap a wooden bead with 4mm red silk ribbon and use the tails of ribbon to attach the bead to the fabric (see page 128).

8 Apply needlelace leaves (see pages 129–132) to the larger embroidered panels.

The top lid panel, showing the use of long and short stitch.

ATTACHING SPANGLES

Spangles are similar to sequins except that they have a small slit in them, which is due to the manufacturing process. Spangles can be stitched down individually with one or several stitches or they can be held in place with a bead or small piece of metal thread known as a 'chip'.

1 Take a single waxed thread in a matching colour and pass the needle through the centre of the spangle. Take your needle down at the edge of the spangle.

2 Come up at the side of the spangle, a third of the way around from the previous stitch and take the needle down through the centre.

3 Secure the spangle in place with a final stitch between the two previous ones, bringing your needle up on one side and back down through the centre of the spangle.

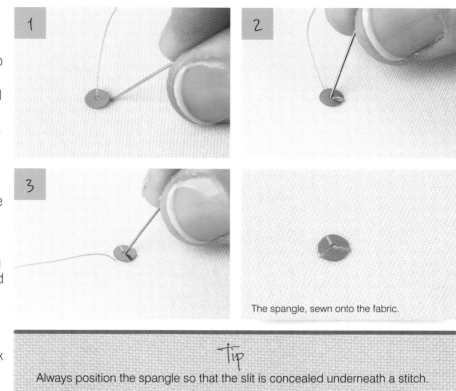

The spangle, sewn onto the fabric.

Tip
Always position the spangle so that the slit is concealed underneath a stitch.

The top front of the casket, with numerous spangles stitched in place.

In the seventeenth century, spangles were often used to decorate embroidered boxes along with men's and women's bodices, gloves and shoes.

WRAPPED BEADS

Wrapped beads give a more raised effect to your embroidery. Wooden beads work best for this, choose ones with a large eye to allow the ribbon to pass through the centre effortlessly.

Beads can be wrapped with either embroidery thread or silk ribbon; however, silk ribbon is more forgiving and covers more quickly. I have used 8mm wooden beads with 4mm silk ribbon wrapped around. If using a larger wooden bead, use a wider silk ribbon.

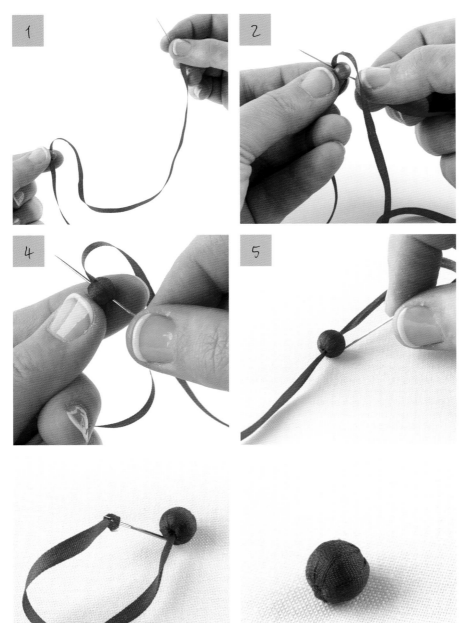

1 Thread a 35cm (13¾in) length of silk ribbon onto a chenille needle and take it through the centre of the bead, leaving a tail of about 5–7cm (2–2¾in). This tail will be used to attach your bead to the fabric.

2 Hold the tail of ribbon in your non-dominant hand and carefully pass the needle through the centre of the bead.

3 Wrap the ribbon around the outside of the bead, then smooth out any wrinkles in the ribbon.

4 Continue to pass the needle through the centre of the bead to cover the entire bead in ribbon. Work methodically around the bead overlapping the ribbon slightly each time, to ensure that the bead is covered. For a neater finish, pull the ribbon tight around the bead.

5 To attach the bead to the fabric, thread the tails of ribbon onto a chenille needle and secure the bead to the background fabric by tucking the needle underneath the bead. Finish the ends of ribbon on the back of your work.

Securing the second ribbon tail under the bead.

The wrapped bead, attached to fabric.

NEEDLELACE LEAVES (SLIPS)

Seventeenth-century embroidered caskets often included many three-dimensional elements – needlelace slips, along with other raised embroidery techniques, were commonly used.

Needlelace slips are pieces of needlelace worked separately before being applied to a design. An outline thread or wire is temporarily stitched down first to act as a framework before the needlelace is stitched within the outline. Buttonhole stitch is commonly used for the needlelace. Needlelace slips are worked on a separate piece of fabric such as calico.

There are eleven needlelace leaves on the stumpwork casket.

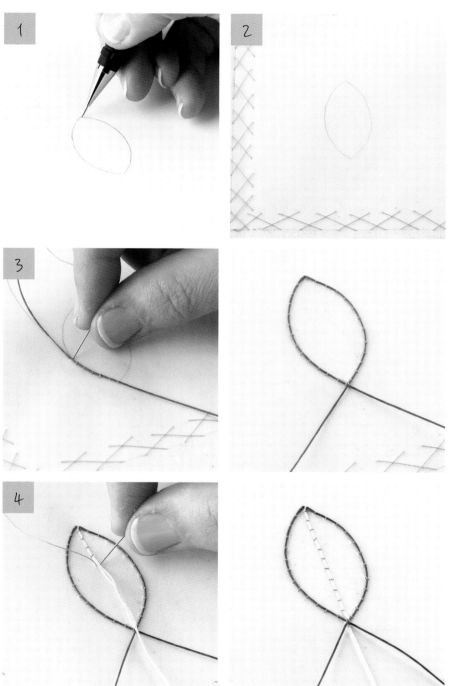

1 Draw a leaf design on tracing paper using a sharp pencil.

2 Place the tracing paper on a piece of calico in a hoop frame. Thread an embroidery needle with some tacking thread and secure the tracing paper to the calico, around the edge of the paper. Oversew around the edges using a herringbone stitch.

3 Thread an embroidery needle with a contrasting colour of tacking thread. Start your thread near the base of the leaf. Place a length of green-paper-covered wire over the design line, leaving a long tail. Couch down the wire around the edge.

4 The needlelace leaf is worked in two separate halves. An additional support thread is stitched down the centre. Wrap a single thread around the wire at the tip of the leaf. Fold the thread in half to create a double thread. Couch the thread down the centre of the leaf. Finish the sewing thread, leaving the tails of thread to be finished off later.

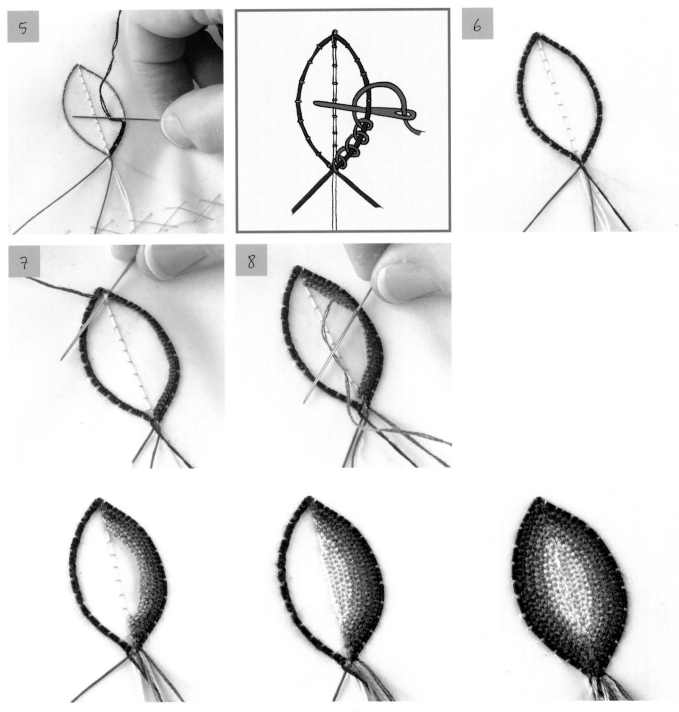

5 Start the needlelace at the base of the leaf. Using two strands in a tapestry needle, make a knot at the end of a long length of thread. Take the needle down through the fabric approximately 4cm (1⁹⁄₁₆in) away from the leaf and bring it back up through the fabric and tracing paper at the base of the leaf. Make your first buttonhole stitch over the wire but not through the fabric or the paper; the tracing paper acts as a smooth surface on which to work the needlelace leaf. See the adjacent diagram (above) for more information on working this stitch.

6 Continue working the first row of buttonhole stitch around the inside of the leaf.

7 The second row and every subsequent row is worked around the edge and looped around the central couched thread before the buttonhole stitch is continued down the same side. Begin the second row in the same way as the first row, passing the thread through the loop of the previous row. When you reach the tip of the leaf, pass your needle around the central vein. This helps to secure the thread.

8 Continue the buttonhole stitch back down to the base of the leaf.

9

Tips

You will need to reduce the number of stitches as you near the centre of the leaf.

Do not make your stitches so tight that it is very difficult to pass your needle through the previous row of stitches.

10

11

12

13

9 When the leaf is completely filled, a tight buttonhole stitch is worked around the edge of the leaf over the wire. Starting at the base of the leaf, bring your needle up on the outside of the wire. Take your needle around the wire, ensuring that the ridge is on the outer edge of the shape.

10 When the leaf is completed, trim away all the knots.

11 Turn the work over and cut all the couching threads.

12 Turn the work over to the front and carefully lift the needlelace leaf away from the tracing paper, leaving any long lengths of thread.

13 Turn on to the back and remove any couching stitches with a pair of tweezers.

APPLYING THE NEEDLELACE LEAF

1 With a stiletto or large chenille needle, make two holes in the fabric at the end of the stem. This is where the wires will be plunged.

2 Carefully pass a wire through each hole in the fabric. Pull the wires to the back so that no wire is visible. Bend the wires back behind the leaf.

3 Thread an embroidery needle onto each end of thread and take it through to the back where the thread finished. There will be a lot of ends to plunge so you do not want them all going through at the same place.

4 Secure these threads on the reverse and trim away any excess thread. Oversew the wire in place and trim away any excess wire.

5 Finally, the central vein is worked in a stem stitch to hold the leaf in place. Using two strands of red stranded cotton in an embroidery needle, start your thread at the base of the leaf working up towards the tip of the leaf.

The needlelace leaf, attached to the fabric.

Notice that I have bent the leaf slightly to give it more movement.

Tip

At step 5, use the tail of the navy thread to stitch over the base of the leaf and secure the leaf to the fabric.

BOX CONSTRUCTION

As with the other handmade boxes, the internal box is constructed first and the external box is built around it. The main internal box comprises a lower section including a drawer, a middle section with three drawers and an additional hidden drawer. The main internal section is completed with an inner top compartment, with an embroidered front and a raised lining.

DRAWER CASINGS

Each drawer has a casing that is made in a similar way to an internal box, with fabric on the inside. The drawer casings give a neat interior finish to the box even when the drawers are removed.

Keep the corners and turnings as flat as possible so that the drawer casings stack neatly together.

1

a

b

c

d

e

DIMENSIONS

BOTTOM DRAWER CASINGS

a) Base: 19.6 x 13.9cm (7¾ x 5½in)

b) Top: 19.6 x 13.9cm (7¾ x 5½in)

c) Back: 19.6 x 3.6cm (7¾ x 1⁷⁄₁₆in)

d) and e) Sides x 2: each 13.7 x 3.6cm (5⅜ x 1⁷⁄₁₆in)

1 Measure and cut the card pieces accurately, using a set square, ruler and sharp pencil. Cover the card pieces in red silk dupion.

The assembled middle and bottom drawer casings.

The bottom, back and sides sewn together.

2 Construct the bottom drawer casing. Ladder stitch the back panel onto the base.

3 Ladder stitch one side panel onto the back panel, then attach the side to the base.

4 Attach the other side panel to the back panel, and then to the base panel.

5 Finally, ladder stitch the top to the back and sides. The back and sides effectively sit within the top and base.

MIDDLE DRAWER CASINGS

The middle drawer casings consist of two separate casings. The left casing holds one drawer. The right casing holds three drawers. This casing is double the width and is divided by a secret drawer (see pages 141–142), held behind two smaller drawers.

1 Measure and cut the card pieces accurately, using a set square, ruler and sharp pencil.

2 Cover the card pieces using the red silk dupion.

3 Construct both of the middle drawer casings in the same way as the bottom drawer casing.

4 Ladder stitch the two middle drawer casings together, so they sit side by side with the narrower one on the left and the wider one on the right. Use a single matching sewing thread in a curved needle.

5 Stack the middle drawer casings on top of the bottom drawer casing, carefully matching up the sides, ladder stitch the drawer casings together. Take care that the sides all sit flush.

DIMENSIONS

LEFT

Top: 6.5 x 13.9cm (2⁹⁄₁₆ x 5½in)

Base: 6.5 x 13.9cm (2⁹⁄₁₆ x 5½in)

Sides x 2: each 13.7 x 4.1cm (5⅜ x 1⅝in)

Back: 6.5 x 4.1cm (2⁹⁄₁₆ x 1⅝in)

RIGHT

Top: 13 x 13.9cm (5⅛ x 5½in)

Base: 13 x 13.9cm (5⅛ x 5½in)

Sides x 2: each 13.7 x 4.1cm (5⅜ x 1⅝in)

Back: 13 x 4.1cm (5⅛ x 1⅝in)

THE TOP COMPARTMENT

The top compartment sits on top of the drawer casings – it is 1cm (⅜in) higher than the external and internal main box. The top compartment has two front pieces: an external front with embroidery – the top fascia, shown on page 119 – and an internal front.

Measure and cut the card pieces accurately, following the dimensions below and using a set square, ruler and sharp pencil. Cover the card pieces using the red silk dupion, with the exception of the front fascia. Follow the method shown for the *Afternoon Tea Box* on pages 103–104 to cover each of the the card pieces – keep in mind that the back and side pieces will be visible when the box is open.

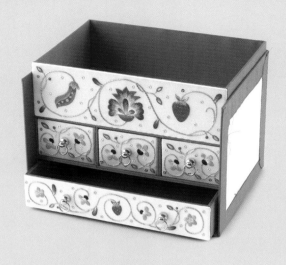

The covered card piece for one side of the top compartment.

DIMENSIONS

Front: 19.6 x 5.6cm (7¾ x 2³⁄₁₆in)

Back: 19.6 x 5.6cm (7¾ x 2³⁄₁₆in)

Sides x 2: each 13.3 x 5.6cm (5¼ x 2³⁄₁₆in)

Base: 19.2 x 13.3cm (7⁹⁄₁₆ x 5¼in)

1 Using a sharp pencil, draw a line on the back of each of the interior side pieces, 1cm (⅜in) from the top edge. This is the line on which the internal box pieces will sit (see page 136).

2 Stick two lengths of double-sided tape to the short sides, keeping the tape below the pencil line.

3 Cut out the fabric following the grain, allowing about 3cm (1³⁄₁₆in) seam allowance at the top.

4 Place the card and fabric face-down on the work surface with the card and trim the bottom corners at 45-degree angles. The top corners are not trimmed back.

5 Fold the fabric to the back along both sides and stick in place, making sure the fabric is pulled taut.

6 Place a piece of double-sided tape along the bottom edge. Cut the corners at 45 degrees, then peel away the backing before securing the tape in place.

7 To achieve neat corners along the bottom edge, first fold the fabric in at the corners using your fingernail. Then fold the fabric up along the bottom edge and stick it in place against the tape.

8 Stick a piece of double-sided tape along the top edge, ensuring that the tape is just below the pencil line (drawn at step 1). This is to avoid any double-sided tape showing through the rising lining, which would cause your curved needle to become sticky.

9 Finally, fold over the excess fabric along the top and pull tight.

Repeat this process for the remaining four pieces.

10 Ladder stitch together all the pieces of the internal compartment then stitch the embroidered top fascia (from page 119) to the front piece.

11 When the top compartment is complete, position it on top of the drawer casings and ladder stitch it in place around all four sides.

ASSEMBLING THE INTERNAL BOX

Once the main drawer casings are constructed, they need to be enclosed in an internal box. The main purpose of this is to extend the front so that the drawer knobs do not interfere with the front doors.

Measure and cut the card pieces accurately, using a set square, ruler and sharp pencil. Cover the card pieces using the red silk dupion.

The full internal box plus casings and internal base.

DIMENSIONS

INTERNAL

Back: 20 x 13.3cm (7⅞ x 5¼in)

Sides x 2: each 15.7 x 13.3cm (6³⁄₁₆ x 5¼in)

Base: 19.8 x 15.7cm (7¾ x 6³⁄₁₆in)

1 Begin by placing the internal base underneath the bottom of the box. The base is longer at the front than the casing is, and needs to be stitched into position along the lower front edge.

2 Using a matching sewing thread in a curved needle, ladder stitch the two pieces together. You may find it easier to tip the box onto its back and work from the top.

3 Position one of the side pieces on the side of the box. Continue your thread and ladder stitch up the front of the box towards the top. Do not stitch the base to the side piece at the moment; this is done later when the other internal side is stitched in place along the front edge.

4 Position the other side piece. Start a new thread at the base of the box and ladder stitch the side to the drawer casings. This can be a little fiddly, but remember to keep your stitches small and tight.

5 Now continue to ladder stitch the internal box pieces together, stitching the back into position.

Do not stitch the sides and back to the raised lining yet; this is stitched later when the lower lid is secured in place and the ribbon stays are inserted between the drawer casing and internal box.

> **Note**
> Note how the internal sides do not go all the way to the top. This is to allow for the lower lid to rest on the internal box.

THE DRAWERS

The drawers are made slightly smaller than the drawer casing to allow them to run smoothly inside the drawer casing. Each of the visible drawers has an embroidered front panel, to which a gold knob with a ring pull is attached. See pages 138–140 for instructions on how to attach the pulls, and pages 141–142 for instructions on constructing the secret drawer.

THE STRUCTURE OF THE DRAWERS

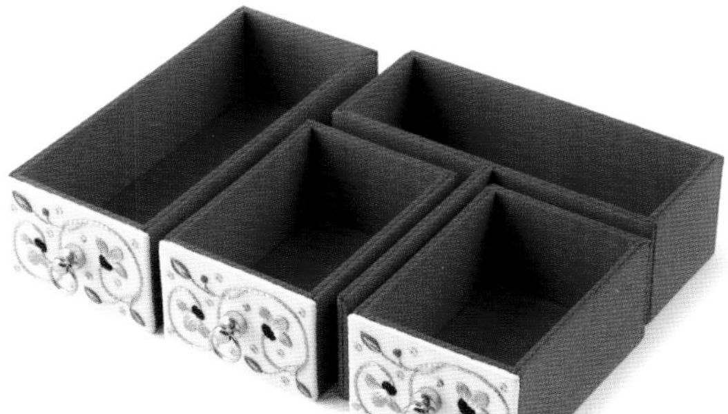

The position of the secret drawer and stem in relation to the three middle drawers.

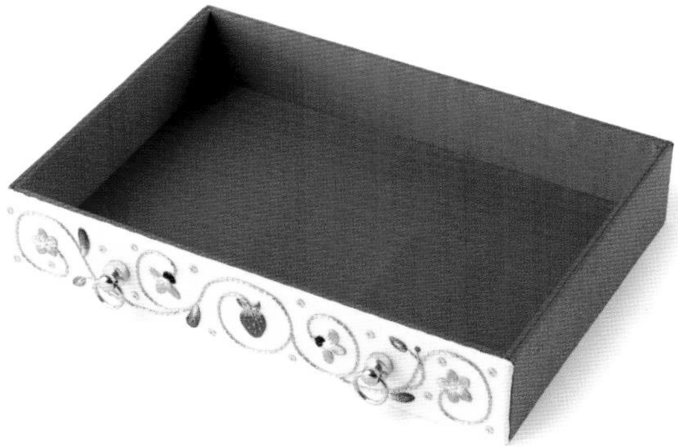

The bottom drawer.

DIMENSIONS

BOTTOM DRAWER

EXTERNAL

Front: 19.1 x 3.5cm ($7\frac{1}{2}$ x $1\frac{3}{8}$in)

Back: 19.1 x 3.5cm ($7\frac{1}{2}$ x $1\frac{3}{8}$in)

Sides x 2: each 13.2 x 3.5cm ($5\frac{3}{16}$ x $1\frac{3}{8}$in)

Base: 18.7 x 13.2cm ($7\frac{3}{8}$ x $5\frac{3}{16}$in)

INTERNAL

Front: 18.7 x 3.3cm ($7\frac{3}{8}$ x $1\frac{5}{16}$in)

Back: 18.7 x 3.3cm ($7\frac{3}{8}$ x $1\frac{5}{16}$in)

Sides x 2: each 12.8 x 3.3cm ($5\frac{1}{6}$ x $1\frac{5}{16}$in)

Base: 18.3 x 12.8cm ($7\frac{3}{16}$ x $5\frac{1}{6}$in)

LEFT DRAWER

EXTERNAL

Front: 6 x 4cm ($2\frac{3}{8}$ x $1\frac{9}{16}$in)

Back: 6 x 4cm ($2\frac{3}{8}$ x $1\frac{9}{16}$in)

Sides x 2: each 13.2 x 4cm ($5\frac{3}{16}$ x $1\frac{9}{16}$in)

Base: 5.6 x 13.2cm ($2\frac{3}{16}$ x $5\frac{3}{16}$in)

INTERNAL

Front: 5.6 x 3.8cm ($2\frac{3}{16}$ x $1\frac{1}{2}$in)

Back: 5.6 x 3.8cm ($2\frac{3}{16}$ x $1\frac{1}{2}$in)

Sides x 2: each 12.8 x 3.8cm ($5\frac{1}{16}$ x $1\frac{1}{2}$in)

Base: 5.2 x 12.8cm ($2\frac{1}{16}$ x $5\frac{1}{16}$in)

CENTRE AND RIGHT DRAWERS (IDENTICAL)

Cut out two of each of these panels:

EXTERNAL

Front: 6 x 4cm ($2\frac{3}{8}$ x $1\frac{9}{16}$in)

Back: 6 x 4cm ($2\frac{3}{8}$ x $1\frac{9}{16}$in)

Sides x 2: each 8.1 x 4cm ($3\frac{3}{16}$ x $1\frac{9}{16}$in)

Base: 5.6 x 8.1cm ($2\frac{3}{16}$ x $3\frac{3}{16}$in)

INTERNAL

Front: 5.6 x 3.8cm ($2\frac{3}{16}$ x $1\frac{1}{2}$in)

Back: 5.6 x 3.8cm ($2\frac{3}{16}$ x $1\frac{1}{2}$in)

Sides x 2: each 7.7 x 3.8cm (3 x $1\frac{1}{2}$in)

Base: 5.2 x 7.7cm ($2\frac{1}{16}$ x 3in)

1 Measure and cut the card pieces accurately, using a set square, ruler and sharp pencil.

2 Cover the card pieces using the red silk dupion, with the exception of the external front.

3 Construct the drawers, omitting the external front.

COVERING THE DRAWER FRONTS

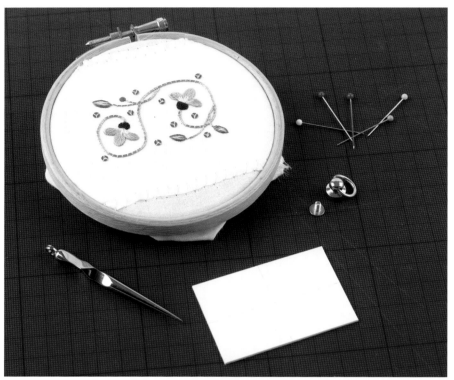

Three of the drawer fronts – for the left, centre and right 'visible' drawers – are the same. Repeat steps 1–19 twice more to create three identical fronts.

A selection of materials and tools for creating the drawer fronts: embroidery hoop mounted with white backed cotton and drawer-front embroidery (see pages 125–126); glass-headed pins, drawer pull, card backing and stiletto.

1 Measure the external drawer front piece along each side to find the centre; mark this with a pencil.

2 Using a pricker, make a small hole in the centre of the drawer front piece.

3 Using a stiletto, reinforce the hole in the centre of the card.

4 Check that the hole is big enough for the screw back.

5 Remove the screw back and sand the card on the reverse to smooth it down. Don't attach the knob to the front of the fabric at this stage as it will get in the way.

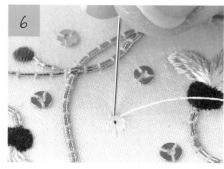

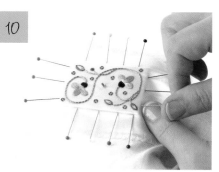

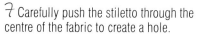

6 With a single sewing thread in an embroidery needle, stitch a double running stitch around the hole in the centre of the embroidered panel (see below).

7 Carefully push the stiletto through the centre of the fabric to create a hole.

8 Remove the embroidery from the hoop. Place the card piece on the reverse of the embroidery and push the screw back through the hole in the card, through to the fabric.

9 Push the screw back all the way through the fabric to the front of the embroidery.

10 Position the embroidery centrally over the card and pin it in place along all four edges.

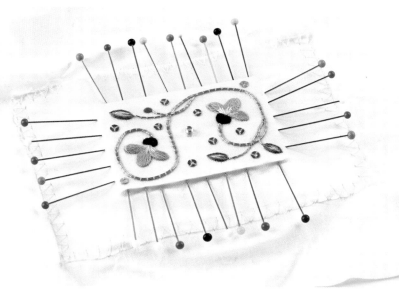

DOUBLE RUNNING STITCH

Also known as Holbein stitch, double running stitch is a very useful stitch. It is used to make a ring of stitches before you cut a hole in your fabric (as at step 6, above). It is identical on both sides of the fabric and helps support the surrounding fabric before inserting a stiletto.

Work the double running stitch slightly bigger than the hole you need, to allow the screw to pass through easily. Keep your stitches small.

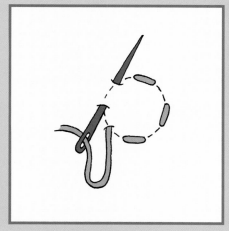

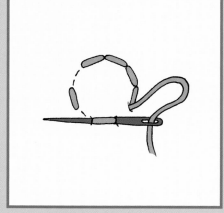

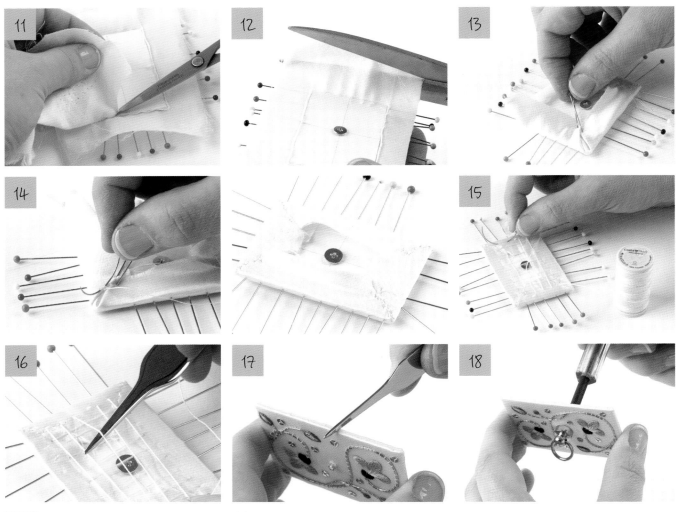

11 Carefully turn over the embroidery. Trim away the backing fabric close to the edge of the card. This will help to reduce the bulk on the back.

12 Trim away the excess fabric around the card, leaving 1.5cm (⁹⁄₁₆in) allowance on each side.

13 Turn in the fabric at the back, mitring the corners. Pin the corners in place.

14 Slip stitch the corners using a matching single sewing thread in a curved needle.

15 Using a buttonhole thread, lace the back (see pages 66–68) – remember to leave the thread on the reel.

16 Use a mellor to tidy and tighten up the lacing.

17 Remove the pins, then remove any pin pricks from around the edge of the drawer front with the edge of the mellor.

18 Screw the drawer pull to the front of the panel and tighten using a screwdriver.

19 Attach the drawer front to the drawer with ladder stitch along all four edges.

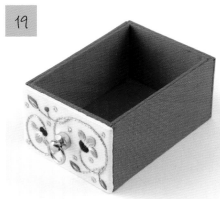

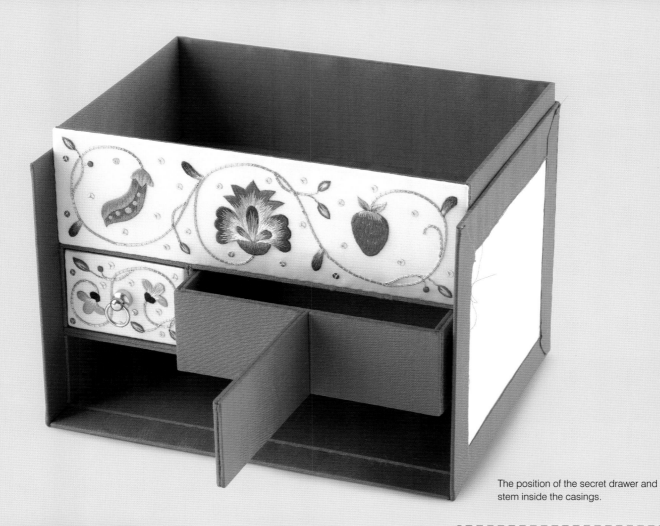

The position of the secret drawer and stem inside the casings.

THE SECRET DRAWER

Seventeenth-century embroidered caskets often had many secret drawers, often concealed behind other drawers to hold any precious items. The secret drawer in this casket is hidden at the back of the right drawer casing. The drawer has a stem attached between two front pieces, which is used to divide the drawer casing and to enable the user to pull out the drawer.

The secret drawer has no embroidery on the front.

DIMENSIONS

EXTERNAL

Front x 2: each 6 x 4cm (2⅜ x 1⁹⁄₁₆in)

Back: 12.5 x 4cm (4¹⁵⁄₁₆ x 1⁹⁄₁₆in)

Sides x 2: each 4.6 x 4cm (1¾ x 1⁹⁄₁₆in)

Base: 12.1 x 4.6cm (4¾ x 1¾in)

Stem x 2: each 8.8 x 4cm (3⁷⁄₁₆ x 1⁹⁄₁₆in)

INTERNAL

Front: 12.1 x 3.8cm (4¾ x 1½in)

Back: 12.1 x 3.8cm (4¾ x 1½in)

Sides x 2: each 4.2 x 3.8cm (1⅝ x 1½in)

Base: 11.7 x 4.2cm (4⅝ x 1⅝in)

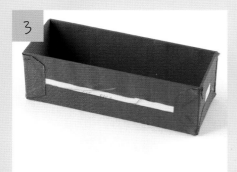

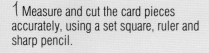

1 Measure and cut the card pieces accurately, using a set square, ruler and sharp pencil.

2 Cover the card pieces using the red silk dupion.

3 Construct the internal drawer.

4 Stitch together the back, sides and base pieces and position around the internal box.

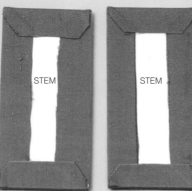

The external front pieces and the stem panels used to pull out the secret drawer.

5 Stitch the two sides of the stem together around all four sides.

6 Stitch the stem to the two front pieces.

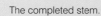

The completed stem.

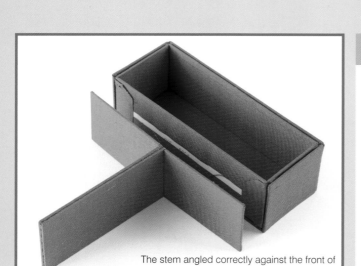

The stem angled correctly against the front of the secret drawer.

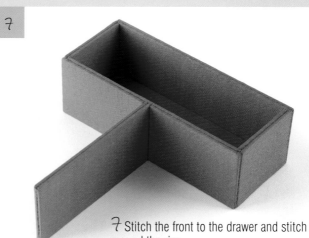

7 Stitch the front to the drawer and stitch around the rim.

The secret drawer is inserted within the internal box and the middle-right hand drawers are inserted either side of the stem.

The constructed internal box with all drawers in place.

ATTACHING THE FEET TO THE BASE

The base has four gold feet attached, one in each corner. These raise the base from the surface, preventing it from getting dirty.

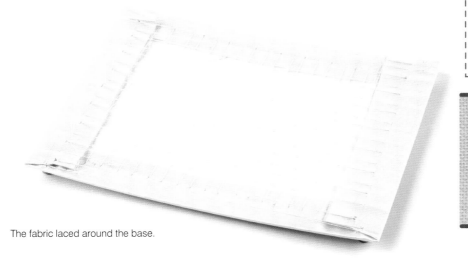

The fabric laced around the base.

DIMENSIONS

Front doors: 10.2 x 13.5cm (4 x 5⁵⁄₁₆in)

Back: 20.5 x 13.5cm (8¹⁄₁₆ x 5⁵⁄₁₆in)

Sides x 2: each 15.9 x 13.5cm
(6¼ x 5⁵⁄₁₆in)

Base: 20.1 x 15.9cm (7¹⁵⁄₁₆ x 6¼in)

Note

The process for attaching the feet to the card piece and to the fabric is identical to the process for attaching the pulls to the drawer fronts – see pages 138–140.

7

1 Measure and cut your card accurately. Mark the position of each foot in the corner of the card by measuring 1cm (⅜in) in from the edge of the card at each corner. Make the marks with a sharp pencil.

2 Make a hole in the card at each corner using a stiletto. Make sure that the hole is big enough for the screw.

3 Mark the position of each foot on the satin fabric, by placing the card over the fabric and marking the foot position through the hole in the card using a fineline pen.

4 Stitch a double running stitch around the foot marking using a single sewing thread, ensuring that the circle is big enough for the back of the foot to pass through.

5 Carefully push the stiletto through the centre of the circle to make a hole.

Repeat for the remaining corners.

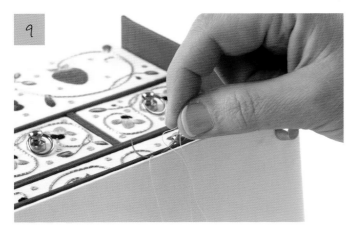

9

6 Position the fabric over the card, matching up the feet markings in each corner. Pin the fabric into place.

7 Push a screw back through the card and fabric from the back. Screw on the foot, ensuring that it is tight.

Repeat the process for the other feet.

8 Fold in the excess fabric to the back of the card and lace the fabric using a buttonhole thread in a curved needle. Remove the pins.

9 Position the base on the base of the box. Stitch the base to the internal box along the front edge.

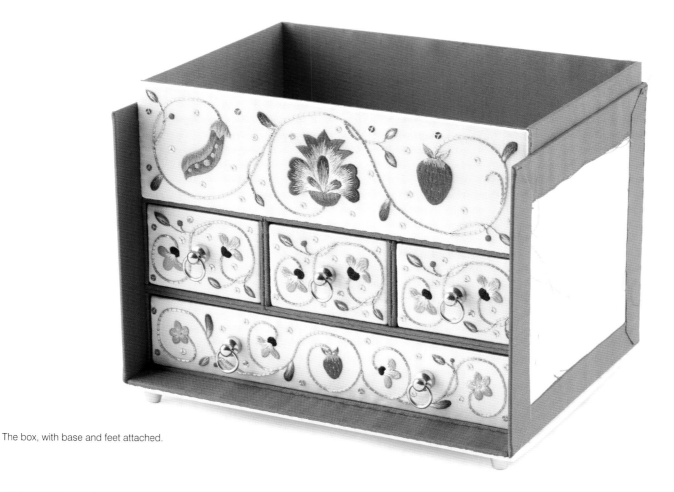

The box, with base and feet attached.

EXTERNAL BOX

The external box has a lockable front door. The front, back and sides are all embroidered.

DIMENSIONS

Front doors: 10.2 x 13.5cm (4 x 5⁵⁄₁₆in)

Back: 20.5 x 13.5cm (8¹⁄₁₆ x 5⁵⁄₁₆in)

Sides x 2: each 15.9 x 13.5cm (6¼ x 5⁵⁄₁₆in)

Base: 20.1 x 15.9cm (7¹⁵⁄₁₆ x 6¼in)

Back panel

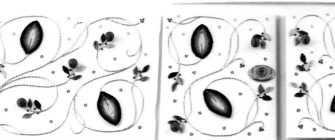

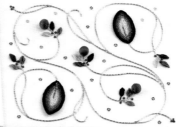

Left side panel   Left door with lock   Right door   Right side panel

The external box panels.

ATTACHING THE LOCK

The lock is attached to the back of the left front door.

1 Find the centre of the embroidery along the right side of the left panel and position the escutcheon (the keyhole component). Mark the position of the keyhole with a hard, sharp pencil (a 3H or 4H) inside the escutcheon.

2 Remove the escutcheon. Using a single sewing thread, work a double running stitch around the outside of the pencil mark (see page 139). Keep your stitches very small. Check that the stitching does not show through the keyhole.

3 Paint on a small amount of PVA (school) glue around the stitched line. This is to help it from fraying when you cut away the keyhole. Allow the glue to dry.

4 Carefully cut away the keyhole using a very sharp pair of scissors. Check that no fabric is remaining inside the keyhole when the escutcheon in positioned on the embroidered panel.

5 Stitch the escutcheon in place securely, using a matching sewing thread in an embroidery needle.

6 Carefully cut a keyhole shape into the card. Once cut, use some sandpaper inside the keyhole to smooth any rough edges.

7 Position the embroidery over the card and pin into position, matching up the keyholes.

8 Lace the embroidery over card, taking care that the lacing stitches do not go across the keyhole.

9 Position the lock on the back of the embroidered panel. Stitch the lock securely in place with buttonhole thread.

ATTACHING THE HINGES

I have used 2cm (¾in) brass hinges on this embroidered casket. It is advisable to source small hinges to complement your box, so as not to interfere with the internal box pieces. Alternatively, you can ladder stitch the seams together twice for extra strength.

The hinges are positioned a hinge-width away from the edge of the card. The fabric has been laced around the card (see pages 66–68) before the hinges are securely attached.

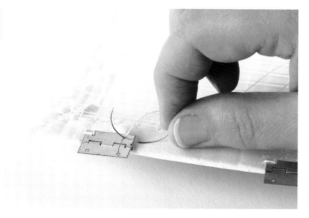

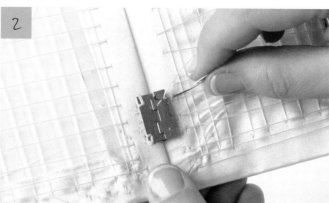

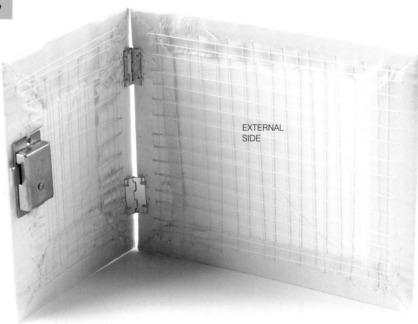

EXTERNAL SIDE

1 Position the hinge on the card approximately 2cm (¾in) from the edge. Using a length of buttonhole thread in a curved needle, securely stitch the hinge into position. Repeat for the other hinge.

2 Line up the door piece with the side piece, ensuring that the top and bottom edges are aligned. Securely stitch the other side of the hinge to the door piece using buttonhole thread in a curved needle. Check that the two pieces open smoothly.

3 The front and side pieces are attached to each other with two brass hinges. The lock is also stitched in place.

MAKING THE LOCK CASINGS

Both doors house a lock casing – the casing on the back of the left-hand door houses the back of the working lock, which interlocks with the 'empty' casing on the right-hand door.

The success of the mortise and its corresponding aperture depends on the accuracy of their positioning. Measure and cut the card pieces accurately, except the mortise panel using a set square, ruler and sharp pencil. Cover the card pieces using the red silk dupion. Construct the lock casing with the exception of the mortise panel.

DIMENSIONS

LOCK CASINGS

Make two casings, one for each door. Each casing comprises:

Top and base: 9.7 x 0.8cm (3¾ x ⁵⁄₁₆in)

Sides x 2: each 12.5 x 0.8cm (4¹⁵⁄₁₆ x ⁵⁄₁₆in)

Back panel: 9.7 x 12.9cm (3¾ x 5¹⁄₁₆in)

The lock mortise and latch panel.

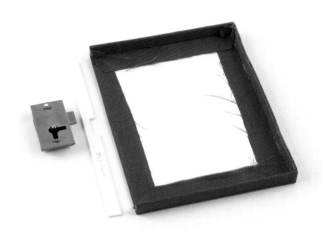

The mortise, latch panel and block casing

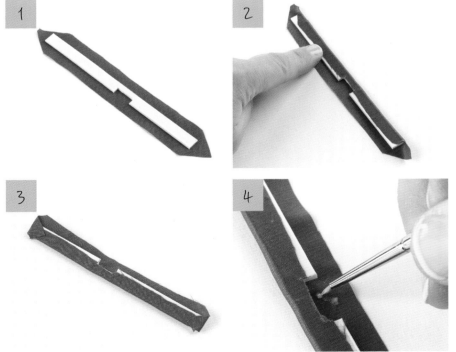

1 Cut out a piece of silk dupion for the latch panel, allowing 1cm (⅜in) seam allowance around each side. Trim away the corners of the silk dupion, taking care not to cut too close to the corners of the card.

2 Place a length of double-sided tape along the long edge of the latch panel. Remove the backing paper. Fold over the fabric and stick in position.

3 Place a piece of tape along each of the ends. Remove the backing paper and fold over the fabric, ensuring that it is pulled taut.

4 To prevent the fabric from fraying when the fabric is cut inside the aperture, paint two lines of glue in a wide 'V'-shape, using a fine paintbrush.

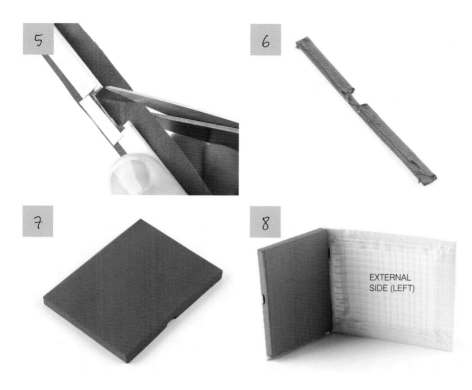

5 Once the glue has dried, cut into the corners of the aperture, following the 'V'-shape. The glue line into the corners should be wide enough that when the fabric is cut, both cut edges are sealed.

6 Place lengths of double-sided tape along the remaining edges of the card. Fold in the fabric ensuring that it is as taut as possible. This can be fiddly, so take extra care to ensure a neat finish.

7 Attach the latch panel to the lock casing to complete.

8 Stitch the casing onto the reverse of the left front door along all four sides.

Repeat the process for the right-hand door. Note that the right side will be a mirror-image of the left side.

EXTERNAL SIDE (LEFT)

ATTACHING THE SIDES

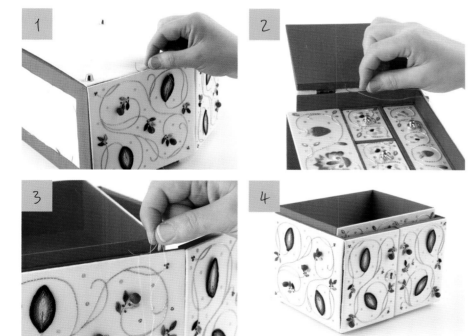

Once both the lock casings are in position, the sides are attached to the base.

1 Turn the box upside-down and rest on some tissue paper to help protect the top of the box. The first side can be positioned and ladder stitched along the bottom edge. Hold it carefully so that the base of the side meets the external base.

2 Turn the box onto its back and ladder stitch the internal side to the external side.

3 Turn the box back onto its base and stitch the internal box to the external box along the top edge.

Do not stitch the raised lining to the internal box at this stage – this will be stitched later when the ribbon stays are positioned.

4 Repeat for the remaining side.

This completes the main part of the casket with the exception of the back panel.

THE LOWER MIDDLE SECTION

The lower middle section sits on the main box. Inside this section is a mirror. It is hinged at the back. Ribbon stays are positioned at each side. The external front, back and sides are all embroidered.

The mirror is stitched to the top piece before the internal box is constructed. Measure and cut the card pieces accurately, using a set square, ruler and sharp pencil. Cover the card pieces using the red silk dupion.

STITCHING THE MIRROR

1

150

3

4

MIRRORED ACRYLIC
Cut to 19.7 x 15.5cm (7¾ x 6⅛in)

EXTERNAL PANELS
Front: 20.5 x 3.5cm (8¹/₁₆ x 1⅜in)
Back: 20.5 x 3.5cm (8¹/₁₆ x 1⅜in)
Sides: both 15.9 x 3.5cm (6¼ x 1⅜in)

INTERNAL PANELS
Front: 20.1 x 3.3cm (7¹⁵/₁₆ x 1⁵/₁₆in)
Back: 20.1 x 3.3cm (7¹⁵/₁₆ x 1⁵/₁₆in)
Sides x 2: each 15.5 x 3.3cm (6⅛ x 1⁵/₁₆in)
Top: 20.1 x 15.9cm (7¹⁵/₁₆ x 6¼in)

1 Cover the internal top using the lacing technique (see pages 66–68).

2 Position the mirror on the internal top piece. The internal top piece is 2mm (¹/₁₆in) larger than the mirror on each side so that the stitching holding the mirror isn't just taken around the card but stitched through the card for added strength.

3 Use a pricker to make small holes into the card where the stitches will be. This makes it a little easier than trying to push a fine needle through the card.

4 Using an 'invisible' (nylon) thread in an embroidery needle, secure your thread in the corner on the reverse. Stitch several times around the mirror, taking your stitching into the hole each time. Be sure that it's secure before finishing the thread on the back.

5 Repeat for the remaining three corners.

Now the internal box can be constructed around the mirror, remembering that the front, back and side pieces sit below the internal top.

The mirror, stitched to the internal top panel.

The internal back panel attached to the top panel.

The completed lower middle section with all panels attached.

The completed lower middle section, upside-down.

ADDING THE RIBBON STAYS

Two ribbon stays – to stop the lid falling too far backwards – are attached to the internal lower lid and inserted between the drawer casings and internal box. Using a matching ribbon 1cm (⅜in) wide, cut each ribbon to a length of 25cm (9¾in).

The positioning of the stays is one third from the back of the box on the base and one third from the front on the lid.

Once the ribbon stays are secured to the internal lower lid, the external front and sides are stitched into position (see below, left).

Ladder stitch around three sides of the rim, making sure the ribbon stays are securely caught into the stitching.

See page 153 for instructions on attaching the other ends of the ribbon stays to the main body of the casket.

Position the ribbon stays against the internal lower lid.

The ribbon stays, stitched in place to the internal lower lid.

ATTACHING THE BACK AND THE LOWER LID

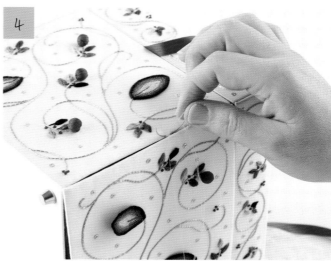

1 Securely attach the hinges to the back panel and the back lower lid (see page 147).

2 Attach the back to the lower lid first. Stitch the side seams first. Stitch the remaining side around the rim of the lower lid, keeping your stitches small.

3 Position the lower lid on the main box.

4 Finally, stitch the back panel into position around all the sides.

Left: the casket with external back stitched in place.

ATTACHING THE RIBBON STAYS

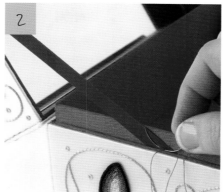

1 Carefully measure the required length of the stay and mark the position with a pin. Place a piece of double-sided tape on each side of the ribbon. Insert the ribbon between the raised lining and the internal box and stick in place. Repeat for the other side, checking that both stays are exactly the same length; readjust if necessary.

2 Ladder stitch the raised lining to the internal box using a matching thread in a curved needle.

The ribbon stays keep the lid from falling back.

UPPER MIDDLE SECTION (LID)

The upper middle section comprises four trapezoid-shaped embroidered panels (see pages 118 and 121) with a box contained inside. The external pieces are higher than the internal pieces, as they sit on an angle. The top lid is fastened with a hook clasp and bar; the position of these is important in order to achieve a neat finish to the lid.

Secure the bar to the front of the trapezoid-shaped piece, checking the position before attaching the internal box. Measure and cut the card pieces accurately, using a set square, ruler and sharp pencil. Cover the internal card pieces using the red silk dupion.

The upper middle section lid. The top section is fastened with a hook clasp and bar mechanism.

DIMENSIONS

Note that for the trapezoid panels (see page 121), the dimensions below relate to the top edge, the bottom edge and the depth (from top to bottom) respectively.

EXTERNAL

Front: 15.2 x 20.5 x 4cm
(6 x 8¹/₁₆ x 1⁹/₁₆in)

Back: 15.2 x 20.5 x 4cm
(6 x 8¹/₁₆ x 1⁹/₁₆in)

Sides x 2: each 11.2 x 16 x 4cm
(4⁷/₁₆ x 6⁵/₁₆ x 1⁹/₁₆in)

INTERNAL

Front: 15.2 x 3cm (6 x 1³/₁₆in)

Back: 15.2 x 3cm (6 x 1³/₁₆in)

Sides x 2: each 10.7 x 3cm
(4³/₁₆ x 1³/₁₆in)

Base: 14.8 x 10.7cm (5³/₄ x 4³/₁₆in)

POSITIONING THE TOP LID

As the external top is at the very top of the casket, it is more pleasing to position the lid over the sides rather than within them.

The internal lid is constructed and covered using double-sided tape (see pages 64–65). Position the top of the lid on the upper middle section. Check that it fits accurately on the top. Ladder stitch it in place with small stitches, using a curved needle.

Finally, to complete the casket, position the upper middle section on the box. Ladder stitch in place.

DIMENSIONS

EXTERNAL

Top: 15.4 x 11.2cm (6¹⁄₁₆ x 4⁷⁄₁₆in)

Front: 15.4 x 2.8cm (6¹⁄₁₆ x 1⅛in)

Back: 15.2 x 2.8cm (6¹⁄₁₆ x 1⅛in)

Sides x 2: each 10.8 x 2.8cm (4¼ x 1⅛in)

INTERNAL

Top: 14.6 x 10.4cm (5¾ x 4¹⁄₁₆in)

Front: 15 x 2.8cm (5¹⁵⁄₁₆ x 1⅛in)

Back: 15 x 2.8cm (5¹⁵⁄₁₆ x 1⅛in)

Sides x 2: 10.4 x 2.8cm (4¹⁄₁₆ x 1⅛in)

The top panel of the lid, prior to final construction.

The top lid prior to its attachment to the main casket.

The top lid, attached to the casket.

Your embroidered casket is now complete. Fill it with your treasures!

The finished casket, with the
doors open.

FURTHER INSPIRATION

I am incredibly lucky to work alongside so many talented embroidery artists at the Royal School of Needlework. Here are just a few examples of their hard work. They demonstrate a wide variety of construction techniques.

I hope the following pages inspire you and provide you with a few ideas for your own embroidered box.

Hexagonal Box
18.5 x 16 x 11.5cm (7 x 6⁵/₁₆ x 4¹/₂in)
Kate Barlow

This hexagonal box is decorated with a spiral of colourful hexagons that have been hand-stitched to the external cotton fabric. The internal fabric is made from patchwork hexagons that have been stitched together. The box has a sit-on lid, and the drawer opens with a hexagonal button pull. The box rests on six small feet constructed from hexagonal pieces of card covered in fabric.

Water Ripple Box

26 x 26 x 14cm (10¼ x 10¼ x 5½in)

Deborah Wilding

The sides of this delightful box open at the top to reveal a movable tray underneath. This box also has two drawers with the added detail of little dragonfly buttons, with a secret drawer hidden behind. The cotton lining fabric contrasts with the blue fabric of the exterior. The box is beautifully embellished with chain stitch, couching, beads and spangles; the dragonflies' wings are made of wired organza.

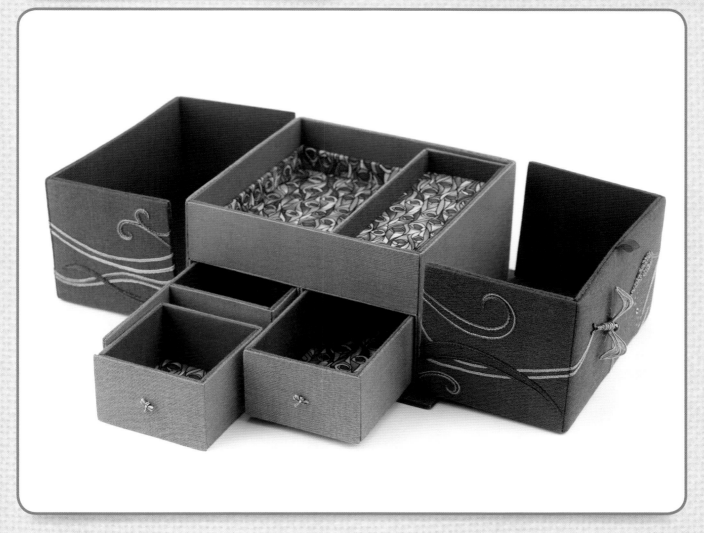

Russian Church
17.5 x 17 x 54cm (6 x 6¾ x 21¼in)

Lisa Bilby

Inspiration for this stunning octagonal box came from the Russian Orthodox churches. It is covered in cream and blue silk dupion. The dome is made from panels of woven pelmet interlining and covered in silk dupion and silk organza. It has been delicately embroidered with gold thread, pearl purl and spangles. The lid lifts off to reveal panels inside, embroidered with small crosses using a gold ophir thread. The box is completed with a cross made from wire wrapped with gold thread, which fits neatly into the top of the box.

Writing Desk
26.5 x 17 x 16cm (10⁷/₁₆ x 6³/₄ x 6⁵/₁₆in)
Nikki Fairhurst

The folding lid on this writing desk is fastened closed using a magnetic clasp, once opened reveals five drawers including a hidden drawer. There is also a removable tray. The calendar indicates the date the box was completed! A cotton fabric with a writing pattern was carefully chosen to decorate the interior, and this has determined the colours used for the rest of the box.

159

'The Jewel in the Crown'
26 x 20 x 27cm (10¹/₄ x 7⁷/₈ x 10⁵/₈in)
Sara Rickards

This silk covered box has been decorated in the style of an English pub, and includes a hanging sign. The front opens to reveal five drawers inside.
Several techniques have been combined to create the embellishment on the front and sides of this box including couching, stitching down gold threads and ribbon embroidered flowers. Raffia has been carefully stitched onto the roof to give an authentic feel to this public house.

GLOSSARY

Appliqué: The technique, in embroidery, of applying fabrics to other fabrics.

Calico: A plain woven cotton fabric.

Circumference: The distance around the edge of a circle.

Couching: A method of stitching down metal or embroidery threads with a finer working thread.

Escutcheon: A flat piece of metal that surrounds a keyhole.

Fusible web: A sheet of adhesive used to bond layers of fabric without the need for sewing.

Goldwork: An embroidery technique that involves the use of metal threads – these can also be imitation gold, silver or copper.

Invisible thread: A very fine thread made from nylon, which blends with any colour fabric.

Mitre: A way of folding fabric around a corner to reduce the bulk and allow the edges to meet evenly.

Ombre ribbon: A shaded silk ribbon, available in different widths.

Organza: A thin, sheer fabric made traditionally from silk.

Passing thread: A metal filament wrapped around a core thread.

Radius: A line from the centre of a circle to the perimeter.

Ribbon embroidery: Embroidery stitches that are worked in silk ribbon.

Spangle: A flat piece of metal, used in metal thread embroidery. It is similar to a sequin in appearance.

Stumpwork: Also known as raised embroidery, a technique whereby the elements of the design are raised from the surface to create a three-dimensional effect. Stumpwork often incorporates beads and wired elements.

Tacking: A temporary stitch usually a running stitch used to hold fabric together or mark outlines on a fabric.

160

INDEX